DAVID LIVERMORE
AND TERRY LINHART

WHAT CAN WE DO?

PRACTICAL WAYS YOUR YOUTH MINISTRY CAN HAVE A GLOBAL CONSCIENCE

DAVID LIVERMORE
AND TERRY LINHART

WHAT CAN WE DO?

PRACTICAL WAYS YOUR YOUTH MINISTRY CAN HAVE A GLOBAL CONSCIENCE

ZONDERVAN.com/
AUTHORTRACKER
follow your favorite authors

ZONDERVAN

What Can We Do?

This title is also available as a Zondervan ebook.
Visit www.zondervan.com/ebooks.

Requests for information should be addressed to:

Zondervan, *Grand Rapids, Michigan 49530*

Library of Congress Cataloging-in-Publication Data

Livermore, David A., 1967-
What can we do? / David Livermore and Terry Linhart.
p. cm.
Includes bibliographical references and index.
ISBN 978-0-310-67035-3 (softcover)
1. Youth in church work. 2. Church group work with youth. 3. Church and social problems—Study and teaching. I. Linhart, Terry, 1964- II. Title.
BV4427.L58 2011
253.0835—dc22 2011006388

Cover design: Micah Kandros
Interior design: David Conn

Printed in the United States of America

---

11 12 13 14 15 16 /DCI/ 23 22 21 20 19 18 17 16 15 14 13 12 11 10 9 8 7 6 5 4 3 2 1

CONTENTS

ACKNOWLEDGMENTS 7
INTRODUCTION 9

PART 1—SEE 13
1. GLOBALIZATION: WHAT IN THE WORLD MATTERS? 15
2. THE VIEW ACROSS THE AISLE: UNDERSTANDING OUR REACTIONS 25

PART 2—LEARN 35
3. "ME? RICH? YEAH, RIGHT!": POVERTY AND HUNGER 37
4. SILENT KILLERS: HIV/AIDS, MALARIA, TB 49
5. SEX AND SOLDIERS FOR SALE: HUMAN TRAFFICKING 59
6. TECHNO-CRAZINESS: TECHNOLOGY AND MEDIA 69
7. "HUG A TREE?!": CARING FOR THE ENVIRONMENT 79
8. INVADED BY ALIENS: IMMIGRATION 91
9. PRIDE AND PREJUDICE: SOCIAL CLASS 101
10. SATAN'S SCHEMES: ETHNIC DIVISION (WITH ERIC IVERSON) 113
11. HOLLYWOOD VERSUS JIHAD: CLASH OF CIVILIZATIONS 125

PART 3—SERVE 135
12. "GLOCAL SERVICE": MAKING A DIFFERENCE NEAR AND FAR 137
13. 15 YEAR OLDS CHANGING THE WORLD 147

EPILOGUE 155
ENDNOTES 157

ACKNOWLEDGMENTS

Thanks to Eric Iverson for his significant contribution to chapter 10 and for all the ways he teaches us as a trusted colleague and friend.

Thank you also to Dave's students and friends at Grand Rapids Theological Seminary who made significant contributions to the following chapters: Carter Sample (chapter 4), Julie Slagter (chapter 5), and Matt Whitacre (chapter 12). It was a joy to share in this project with you.

Thanks to Jay Howver at Youth Specialties not only for inviting us to do this project, but also for sharing a commitment to these global issues with us. And thank you to Roni Meek and Dave Urbanski for their editorial partnership in actually seeing this to completion with us.

Thanks to Mark Root of the Bowen Library at Bethel College for his research support, to Katie Weiss and Mark Matlock for their helpful information, and to Dan Gutwein and Derry Prenkert for their experienced input. Thanks to the administration of Bethel College (Indiana) for Terry's writing sabbatical and opportunity to expand his own global awareness.

Most importantly, thank you to our wives—Linda Livermore and Kelly Linhart—for their continued support, encouragement, and shared interest in making a difference in the world.

INTRODUCTION

Nearly 30 million people watched the 2007 YouTube video of Caitlin Upton, Miss Teen South Carolina, attempting to answer the following question: "Recent polls have shown a fifth of Americans can't locate the U.S. on a world map. Why do you think this is?" Caitlin replied,

> I personally believe that U.S. Americans are unable to do so because, uhmmm, some people out there in our nation don't have maps and uh, I believe that our, I, education like such as, uh, South Africa, and uh, the Iraq, everywhere like such as, and I believe that they should, uhhh, our education over here in the U.S. should help the U.S., uh, should help South Africa, it should help Iraq the Asian countries so we will be able to build up our future, for us.[1]

Painful to relive that wince-worthy answer, isn't it?

We've often defended youth as being far more globally conscious than the older generations in the church. We wanted to believe Caitlin was merely experiencing stage fright. And in fact, Caitlin offered that very explanation a few days later on the *Today* show while also providing a much more coherent response. But the question remains: Does it matter that many of our students are far more aware of the latest episode of *American Idol* and *Glee* than they are of what's going on in the *real* real world?

Pundits had a field day with Caitlin's misfire. Surely this proved the demise of our youth. But before we too quickly ridicule an 18-year-old girl for botching an answer to a live question posed over the airwaves in the Miss Teen USA Pageant, recent research among American *adults* reveals:

- Only two of five voters can name the three branches of the federal government.
- Only one in seven can find Iraq on a world map.
- Only one in five knows we have 100 U.S. senators.

But more than half of American adults can identify at least two members of *The Simpsons* family from television.[2]

Okay—so American adults and students don't score very well on global consciousness. Is that really such a big deal? For students navigating social pressures, enduring the pain of blended families, discovering their own identities, and fighting off depression, is finding the United States, much less Iraq, on a world map really that important? And does understanding the ins and outs of immigration or discussing the ethical complexities of globalization really have a place in youth ministry?

Yes.

In fact, to ignore these pressing topics works against effective discipleship. The following are a few reasons why:

- *Perspective*: With our increasingly interconnected world, these global issues are shaping what occurs in your youth room, albeit often subconsciously. Responding well begins with opening our eyes to what's going on in the world both near and far.
- *Integrate Faith with Global Issues*: Many youth care deeply about the world, and they're getting lots of input from other sources about how they should be involved. Youth ministry should help students see how their faith intersects with issues such as poverty, immigration, and the environment.
- *Respond*: Youth often hear alarming statistics about global issues but have no ways to respond. Churches should be at the forefront of offering solution-oriented responses for how youth can make a difference today.
- *Future*: Over the next decade, our youth will be going to college or starting careers and beginning families. By discipling them in light of these global issues, we have the opportunity to make a generational impact as future adults make a difference in the world through their relationships, interests, and careers.

While global issues have deep ethical implications for youth at home and abroad, they're seldom discussed in many youth ministries. It's difficult to keep up with all the trends, but there are things we can do. Whether through a short-term mission experience, pulling a story from the BBC News, or discussing a movie such as *Slumdog Millionaire*, you have the chance to prepare your students for lifelong engagement with the pressing issues of our day. That's the purpose of this book—to help you grow in global awareness, learn about underlying issues, and provide you with some practical ideas and resources to help you better lead your youth to live their Christian faith in the context of today's world.

Our children and adolescents are growing up in a global world that's as close as their fingertips. They can text their friends in China, watch worldwide events on their cell phones, and purchase the latest fashion from Australia—all while driving down a country road in Oregon. If we're truly discipling teens to live their Christian faith in the 21st-century world, then encountering global issues and examining them in light of the gospel is essential.

Plainly speaking, the days of believing we can ignore global issues are over. *We no longer have the luxury of viewing our wants and needs apart from those of the rest of the world.* The shoes we wear, the foods we eat, the high-tech toys we buy, and the companies in our towns are all intertwined with our fellow human beings living on the other side of the world—and we must prepare teens to live generously among them. We need to help them connect their deepest longings and dreams with the world's needs. And we have to ask these kinds of questions: *How does the gospel intersect with human trafficking, genocide, and war? And what can a single youth ministry possibly do about it?* What can we do?

The answer? Quite a bit.

That's also what we'll explore together in these pages.

Over the next several chapters, we'll give you a glimpse of what it might look like for your youth ministry to more fully engage globally. We'll share the findings from some of our research and global work, offering perspectives on some of the key issues facing today's world.

Part 1 begins with some overarching perspectives we need to keep in mind before discussing some specific global realities. Part 2 provides an overview of nine global concerns facing our generation and offers some practical ways for youth ministries to respond. While it's impossible to comprehensively cover all of today's issues, we have addressed some of the most essential ones and have suggested some ways they relate to your ministry—both for your teens today and in the years ahead. Part 3 gives some concluding guidelines for how we should serve with our youth locally and globally.

Both of us are on a journey to understand how these global realities should intersect with our own families, work, and churches. And we've had the rich privilege of encountering many other youth workers around the world who are making a world of difference by giving attention to the kinds of concerns outlined in this book.

So thanks for joining us in the adventure of making a world of difference in and through the teenagers in your life.

PART 1

SEE

Preparing to serve our neighbors near and far begins with *seeing* what lies beyond our borders. We'll start with a brief overview of globalization and its implications for Christian youth. (We won't bombard you with statistics, but it's helpful to get a 30,000-foot view before jumping into some of the more specific issues addressed in part 2.) Then we'll consider the unique perspectives we each bring to conversations on these topics. Since our different upbringings, networks of friends and family, and political assumptions play a big role in shaping how we each think about and respond to these realities, it's important to acknowledge the importance of our uniquenesses.

What can we do? Come with us . . . and *see* what lies beyond the borders of your world.

CHAPTER 1

GLOBALIZATION

WHAT IN THE WORLD MATTERS?

When I (Dave) was a teenager in youth group, international travel and exotic experiences were reserved for the rich and famous, soldiers, and missionaries. Most of my global understanding came from visiting missionaries who told me fascinating stories about life in the jungle, language struggles, and discovering exotic foods.

Today, it's a rare youth group that hasn't crossed an international border to experience many of these things firsthand. It's an overused cliché . . . but the world has gotten smaller. Many North Americans blow across international borders like we used to go from state to state or province to province. And even if you rarely travel far from home, other nations are literally moving in next door.

Both of us have had the unique privilege of doing quite a bit of international travel. We've gone on countless mission trips with high school groups, conducted research overseas, and we continue to engage in work with leaders around the globe. But increasingly we're finding that we don't even have to leave home to experience the wonders of globalization—the growing interdependence of people throughout the world. Through transportation and communication advancements, we—the 6.8 billion people on the planet—are more closely tied together than ever before. It's amazing how life in our rapidly globalizing planet brings us an unprecedented number of encounters with people, places, and issues from around the world.

IT'S A FLAT, FLAT, FLAT WORLD

Journalist Thomas Friedman popularized the phrase *the world is flat* to suggest that the competitive playing fields between industrialized and emerging markets are leveling. For a long time there was a sense that people in China and Mexico, for example, were waiting for a German or U.S. company to come charging in to build factories and create jobs; today, Chinese and Mexican firms are building their own factories and often outselling their Western counterparts. In the new millennium, all business is global.[1]

The other day I (Dave) was slogging through a bunch of administrative tasks in preparation for an overseas trip. While responding to an email from a ministry partner in China, a friend in Malaysia sent me an instant message asking, "Can we Skype?" As I moved the cursor to the reply icon, I noticed a "breaking news" alert in my Web browser, and it updated me on some of the latest violence in Sudan. At that moment I had more information about some of the happenings in Africa than I typically receive about my kids' progress in school, just three blocks away.

Such is life in the so-called flat world.

Anyway, I got through most of my email and even managed to catch up with my friend in Malaysia for a few minutes over Skype. I had just enough time to pick up my wife Linda for a lunch date at our favorite Indian restaurant in Grand Rapids. (Admittedly western Michigan isn't flush with choices for Indian cuisine, but the food and ambiance at Bombay Cuisine is great.)

After lunch we made a quick stop at the grocery store. The guy bagging our stuff was a refugee from Sudan. He was very gaunt; his bones nearly poked through his skin. We've talked before. I wondered if it would be appropriate to ask for his view of the latest happenings in Sudan. I decided to keep things at the small-talk level. When I got home, I made a quick phone call to inquire about a charge that showed up on our credit card bill last month. The customer service representative picked up from a call center in India. A few minutes later I was on my way to my girls' school and arrived just in time to pick them up from the day's Cinco de Mayo celebration.

This is life in the flat world.

We're connected to grieving civilians in Gaza, starving people in Burundi, and women trafficked for sex in Thailand. Many of us sponsor children through monthly donations and read Facebook posts from people living a dozen time zones away. Although such connectivity brings with it a certain "cool" factor, more importantly it asks us to take responsibility for people not just in our homes or neighborhoods or schools or churches—but people everywhere. So throughout the book, we'll take on several key, world-shaking issues and suggest several practical ways we can respond to them.

But before tackling some of the issues one by one, we want to view our increasingly borderless world as a whole—to look through a wide-angle lens to see the seamless connections between people, issues, and places near and far. We'll start by looking at our global village and then consider three of the most important issues of globalization we need to understand—economics, youth, and Christianity.

ONE VILLAGE

A wide-angle view begins with a snapshot of our global village. Today's population is racing toward 7 billion people.[2] If all of us populating this planet lined up single file, we'd create 112 lines circling the globe. That's a mind-blowing thought and difficult to grasp. So another way to get a glimpse of today's world is to imagine what it would look like if all the realities of our globe were represented in a single global village of 100 people. If that were the case, here's how it would break down:

- The village consists of 60 Asians, 14 Africans, 12 Europeans, 8 Latin Americans, 5 people from the USA and Canada, and 1 person from the South Pacific.
- 51 are male; 49 are female.
- 82 are people of color; 18 are white.
- 80 live in substandard housing.
- 67 are non-Christians; 33 are Christians.
- 67 are illiterate.
- 50 are malnourished and 1 is dying of starvation.
- 39 have no access to improved sanitation.
- 33 have no access to safe water supplies.
- 33 receive and attempt to live on only 3 percent of the village's income.
- 24 don't have any electricity (and of the 76 who do have electricity, most use it only for light at night).
- 7 have access to the Internet.
- 5 control 32 percent of the entire village's wealth—and each of those 5 is a U.S. citizen.
- 1 has a college education.
- 1 has HIV.[3]

We'll unpack several of these realities throughout the book. The most important consideration for now is being aware of the interconnectedness of our lives and ministries with what's going on globally. Because your youth have the potential to meet certain needs in our global village. And in turn, the people in our village offer many resources for discipling teenagers.

ONE ECONOMY

Globalization is eroding economic borders. When most people use the word *globalization*, they're talking about international business. It involves more than that, but it's with good reason that Nike, Sony, Billabong, and Coca-Cola are among the first images that come to mind when we think about globalization. Many of us have welcomed the familiar taste of Coke in a faraway village on a short-term mission trip. Coke is available in more places around the world than any other product. In fact, many large multinational corporations like Coca-Cola have more financial holdings than entire nations do. Then again, in our flat world nowadays you can just as easily be involved in global business as a solo entrepreneur working from a home office as someone working for a massive multinational company. In response, there are many questions we should be asking ourselves, such as: *What ethical implications should this raise for how we shop? What regulations should governments place upon large corporations? What's the relevance of this understanding to youth ministry?*

Our youth and their parents are deeply impacted by globalization—as consumers, employees, movie fans, etc. Most North Americans used to be all for globalization, usually without even knowing it. Globalization allowed us to buy things for a lot less money. Buying a pair of jeans made by a sweatshop worker in Bangladesh earning 25 cents per hour instead of a pair of jeans made by someone in Cleveland making $8 per hour "benefits" us financially. For years a vocal minority—usually outside Evangelicalism—protested the sweatshops, exploitive labor practices, and corporate greed often involved with outsourced manufacturing. But global competition is an inevitable outcome of capitalism. Why wouldn't a business find the cheapest place to make their products in order to increase profits?

As more and more North Americans have lost jobs in recent years to overseas counterparts in China, Mexico, and India, more Americans have begun to question whether globalization was such a good thing after all. The economic challenges aren't obvious when it's *your* country that benefits. But now with China possessing a growing stake in the world of business, for example, some Americans are feeling the threat of China taking over the world—not dissimilar to how other countries used to fear the U.S. and its influences.

And when an economic crisis hits, like the one in 2008, it shows we're forever connected economically with each other. Globalization isn't going away, so we need to pay attention to the long-term impact of so many complex issues related to the globalization of business.

For example, the establishment of call centers in cities such as Bangalore and Delhi has brought unprecedented economic opportunities to many Indians—in fact, the Indian middle class is now equivalent in size to the entire U.S. population. Yet 700 million Indians remain desperately poor, and many allege that globalization widens the disparity between the rich and the poor. No simple answers exist for challenges like these.

Or consider the fair trade coffee movement, which charges extra for a pound of "fair-trade" coffee in order to pay coffee farmers a fair price for their coffee beans rather than gouging them. It's a great idea with lots of momentum behind it from big-name coffee shops such as Starbucks and Caribou. However, many critics maintain that the vast majority of the extra profits gained from additional fees for a cup of fair-trade coffee go to the businesses and fair-trade coffee promoters, not the farmers. Some argue that you'd do far more to help coffee farmers by buying "non-fair trade" coffee and donating the difference to a nonprofit organization devoted to helping oppressed farmers in Guatemala.[4]

There aren't simple answers to these dilemmas, but we do promise to give you some concrete ways to respond throughout the coming chapters. (In particular, chapter 3 specifically addresses the issue of poverty and global economics.) For now, our primary concern is to broaden your perspective to see the reality of our global economy and begin thinking about the implications for how you disciple your students.

ONE YOUTH

Imagine Web cam images from teenagers' bedrooms in Atlanta, Mexico City, Tokyo, and Stockholm. Do you think you could tell the bedrooms apart? Several years ago, a New York City-based ad agency filmed teenagers' rooms in 25 countries. The congruencies in their bedrooms were striking. Basketballs sat next to soccer balls and closets were stuffed with what appeared to be the global adolescent uniform: baggy Levi's or Diesel jeans, NBA jackets, and Doc Martens and Timberland shoes. "In a world divided by trade wars and tribalism, teenagers, of all people, are the new unifying force. From the steamy playgrounds of Los Angeles to the stately boulevards of Singapore, kids show amazing similarities in taste, language, and attitude . . . Propelled by mighty couriers like MTV, trends spread with sorceress [sic] speed . . . Teens almost everywhere buy a common gallery of products: Reebok sports shoes, Procter & Gamble Cover Girl makeup, Sega and Nintendo videogames, Pepsi, etc."[5]

Of course if this study were conducted today, it would reveal a different array of logos and products. And although New York and Paris used to be the epicenters of youth culture, Mumbai, Tokyo, and Shanghai are as much the driving centers of youth culture today for most of the world's youth. And more and more youth are connecting with peers worldwide through a common language of music, movies, fashion, and pop culture.

A word of caution is in order, however. We used to be among those who would talk about the unifying world of youth by suggesting that teenagers in Dubai, Prague, and Chicago may have far more in common with each other than any of them have in common with their own parents. There's some truth to that. But we can't discount the profound cultural differences that still exist among youth from various places around the world. There *are* some interesting similarities between youth in Toronto, Tampa, and New Delhi—but venture into the tribal communities outside Chiang Mai, Thailand or Monrovia, Liberia, and suddenly the unifying youth culture seems nearly nonexistent.

Keep in mind that barely 29 percent of people in the world have ready access to the Internet[6], and that "youth culture" is largely a middle class, urban phenomenon. Most teenagers worldwide have never talked on the phone, believe it or not, much less dabbled in Facebook accounts and instant messaging. And while it's true that a uniform, global culture characterizes growing numbers of youth around the world, alongside that reality are many youth who still have very little in common with the youth we encounter week to week. Regardless, global youth are one of the most targeted markets by a growing culture of business and consumerism—sadly it's not just because they're primary target consumers, but also because they're a primary labor source.

Researcher Jennifer Gidley has studied global trends happening to youth in places around the world. One trend she identifies is the way teens' imaginations are being colonized by MTV, iTunes . . . and al-Qaeda. Toys are no longer made for kids and their parents; they're made by industries that want to create appetites for long-term consumers. And—on the other side of the coin—youth are often the top suicide-bombing recruits. Everyone wants a piece of adolescents.

In addition, culture is increasingly being secularized. More and more human explanation of the unexplainable is viewed as superior to the supernatural, spiritual rationales in Christian, Hindu, Muslim, and Jewish contexts. And youth—more than anyone else—will be impacted by the degradation of the environment.[7]

These global trends are reason for concern.

But not everything going on among global youth is bad news. Criticism of youth has been a consistent theme across history. Each generation seems to blame and fear the younger generation coming up, and soon that once-younger generation becomes adults who do the same thing. Instead we need to be more accurate in how we talk about today's global youth. We can't say today's adolescents are "so much worse" than those growing up 30 years ago. Research just doesn't support that. Believe it or not, most high school students in North America are making safer choices today than their counterparts did 30 years ago.[8] And this better decision-making is mirrored by youth in other countries as well. For instance, U.S. high school students are more apt to wear seatbelts, avoid getting into cars with drivers who've been drinking, and drink less alcohol than teenagers did 15 years ago. And on a global level, tobacco and pot and methamphetamine use, as well as sexual intercourse, are in decline among youth, though some regions have seen slight increases.[9] Probably the most encouraging news about U.S. youth is that attempted suicide among high school students continues to decline, a welcome change from the sharp upswing in the 1970s and early 1980s.

No one is sure why these healthier trends exist. Is it possible that globalization is playing a *positive* role in the lives of many youth? Three global developments may offer us some insight. First, young people today know more than ever before. Better education has had a significant impact on the reduction in risky behavior because it provides hope. Where there isn't education, adolescents take greater risks. More young people than ever are graduating from high school, many of whom go on to college, a predictor of a more hopeful outlook.[10] And the quality of education is improving in most places globally. It's still not enough, but the results are promising.

In addition, many local governments, parents, schools, and faith communities are more involved in the lives of youth than in previous generations. Think about the available number of parenting classes, books, and Web sites. Countless schools have adopted special rules regarding how students are to treat other students (e.g., zero tolerance on bullying), and many communities around the world offer a variety of youth programs. Talk shows champion a child-centered focus that never used to exist. Globalization is raising the expectations of parents and their kids.

Finally, adolescence extends longer and to more places than ever before. Historically, most individuals have gone directly from childhood to adulthood. But ongoing development in health and education allows more people to experience the transitional phase of adolescence. In many contexts, the teen "years" now extend well into one's twenties—a period known as "emerging adulthood."[11] This extension of adolescence can be both a blessing and a curse. But the aforementioned developments are ways this transitional phase can be meaningful.[12]

Therefore, on the whole, when compared to adults and previous generations of youth over the last 40 years, adolescents today take fewer risks and are more conventional in their thinking. Youth workers don't often hear that most students make it through adolescence very well, possess positive identities, and have hopeful outlooks on the future.

At the same time, though, there are still many at-risk youth around the world. In fact, despite the positive trends among youth worldwide, problems for at-risk youth seem more pronounced. There is still a great need for programs that reach out to these adolescents. Way too many kids in urban contexts continue to fall through the cracks, as do lots of kids in more rural communities around the world. But globalization is offering growing numbers of youth an "out" from the local pressures. Connecting to a larger world provides a broader perspective and hope for a better future.

We deal with the issues of global youth ministry much more thoroughly in our book, *Global Youth Ministry*.[13] For now, in taking this panoramic view of globalization, it's important to note the ways youth in particular are affected by the issues of our borderless world. Even though there's a global youth culture emerging from one end of the planet to the other, we're wise to see it as a mile wide and an inch deep. Youth in Tokyo are profoundly different from youth in Beijing and Vancouver. But they're also connected. They're products of globalization more than any other generation before them, a reality that is both reason for celebration and concern.

ONE CHURCH

The interconnectedness of our globalized world also applies to what's occurring throughout the Christian faith. It's easy to hear the evening news and read many mission reports and feel pretty discouraged about the vitality of the Christian church. Though we face many challenges, the church is growing faster than ever before in world history.[14] On average, two more people surrender their lives to Jesus every second—and *most* of that growth happens outside North America and Western Europe. That's one of the biggest shifts from the last few years.

Two centuries ago, 99 percent of Christians lived in North America and Western Europe. Throughout the 1800s, many Christian denominations, particularly in Europe, became more aggressive in their mission efforts. By 1900, about 90 percent of Christians were living in North America and Western Europe. The influence of Christian mission was felt in Latin America, Africa, and Asia. But during the next 100 years, however, a massive shift occurred. By 2000, nearly 70 percent of the Christian church was living *outside* North America and Western Europe. This shift is due, in part, to the slower growth of Christianity in the West. But it's more the result of the fast-paced growth in what's often called the "Southern Church" or the "Global South" (i.e., Central and South America, Southern Africa, Southern India, and Southern China).

Just now, two more people surrendered their lives to Jesus. And two more. And two more. It keeps happening every second!

And you and your youth are connected to it.

The typical Christian today is said to be a woman living in a Nigerian village or Brazilian favela.[15] We celebrate the rapid growth of the Christian church in places like Nigeria and Brazil, and we also need to acknowledge that this growth isn't entirely separate from our own church experiences. Because nearly all churches across North America share interesting connections with believers in other parts of the world. The Christian church is connected like never before.[16]

As we tackle global issues, we do so with our brothers and sisters in Christ scattered around the world. Many of the issues we'll encounter in part 2 of this book—from poverty to HIV/AIDS to human trafficking—are daily realities for many of our brothers and sisters in Christ.

FINAL THOUGHTS

The escalating number of short-term mission trips is largely a result of globalization. It's never been easier or more economical to get from one side of the world to the other. We have plenty of concerns about how to do short-term missions well, but one of its greatest benefits is how it can enhance our understanding of life for people in other parts of the world. We encounter many global realities first-hand during trips to the south side of Chicago, Mexico, or Kenya, and students often return home with a passion for doing something about what they've witnessed. The opportunities to see these realities up close bring us unprecedented opportunity and responsibility to live out the gospel near and far.

Imagine that Devon, a citizen in our global village, is the proud owner of a very rare and valuable old luxury sports car—a Bugatti. It's so rare that no insurance company will touch it. Devon's Bugatti is his pride and joy. In addition to the pleasure Devon gets from driving and caring for his car, he knows its rising market value means he'll always be able to sell it and live comfortably after retirement.

One day when Devon is out for a drive, he parks the Bugatti near the end of an abandoned railway track and goes for a walk along the track. As he does so, he sees that a runaway train, with no one aboard, is barreling down a parallel track. Looking in the opposite direction, he sees the small figure of a child playing in a tunnel who will very likely be killed by the train. He can't stop the train, and the child is too far away to remove from danger, but Devon can throw a switch that would divert the train down an alternate track—the track upon which his Bugatti is parked. If he throws the switch, nobody gets killed—but the train would destroy his Bugatti. Thinking of his joy in owning and driving his car, and the financial security it represents, Devon decides against throwing the switch. As a result the child is killed. But for many years to come, Devon enjoys owning his Bugatti and the financial security it represents.[17]

The choices we make from the comforts of our homes affect our fellow image-bearers around the world. Together, we can throw a switch and spare the lives of people near and far. But doing so requires sacrifice and probably will mean some discomfort. But it's at the core of what it means to be a faithful disciple of Jesus today.

Maybe you're not convinced? That's okay. We want to journey together to see how our lifestyles and choices shape the lives of people around the world. And we want to help our youth do the same—not only today, but as we prepare them for a lifetime of living beyond borders.

CHAPTER 2

THE VIEW ACROSS THE AISLE

UNDERSTANDING OUR REACTIONS

Twenty years ago, most North American Christians spent very little time talking about subjects such as poverty, HIV/AIDS, immigration, and the need for clean water. These issues were seen as peripheral and potential distractions from the gospel. Today, however, almost every youth ministry is looking for ways to respond to people's physical needs locally and globally. Even many of the most conservative evangelical churches and youth ministries are getting involved in compassion and development efforts alongside their evangelistic pursuits.

What changed?

In some cases this shift came about as Christian leaders thoughtfully studied the Scriptures, traveled on short-term mission trips, and saw the importance of living out the gospel in word and deed. But in far more cases, it's come as a result of a cultural shift in North America where key leaders and churches have told us we need to get involved in these kinds of issues. This isn't coming only from the Shane Claibornes. It's voiced from leaders such as Rick and Kay Warren, Tony Evans, and Tim Keller.

We're excited about this shift. The gospel isn't very good news if it doesn't touch the very real needs of people and communities around the world. But as we interact with youth leaders about the kinds of issues covered in this book, we get varied responses. Many share our concerns and interests, some fear getting one more guilt trip without any practical solutions, and others fear these are more politically driven concerns than something that really ought to be central to the work of youth ministry. We're sympathetic to all those responses. So before we address some key global realities in part 2, let's step back and think about the reasons for the varied responses to getting involved beyond our borders. We need more than bandwagon activism if we're going to effectively disciple youth to respond to worldwide realities. It requires a thoughtful engagement that intentionally sees the connection between our upbringings, our surroundings, and our theologies with how we respond to the issues of our day.

WE WATCH. WE LEARN. WE COPY.

From the moment we're born, we're taught to see the world in a certain way. Of course, most of this socialization process occurs subconsciously. Our parents teach us what's "normal" and what's "weird." We're quickly given a sense of right versus wrong and success versus failure. Our childhood networks expand to include extended family, neighbors, and school friends, and our views of the world are developed further. Usually these individuals reinforce what we've been learning at home. We're taught good and bad manners, what it means to be a man or woman, and how to get ahead in life. Then we watch for cues about how to act and what the consequences are for those who don't conform. As we continue through high school and go on to college or the working world, we continue to learn from people around us what's cool, important, and right. We watch, we learn, and we copy.

The vast majority of people in the world can be described as conformists. Most individuals make choices about where to live, how to dress, what car to drive, and where to vacation based upon the leanings of the dominant groups to which they belong. This decision-making style carries over to their views on politics, faith, and culture. Conformists want what "their" groups value. They feel trust and warmth with people like themselves and feel uncomfortable and suspicious of people who are different. Even so-called "alternative" groups usually conform to the agendas and styles of other alternatives in their subcultures. For example, many emergent church leaders hang out with, sound like, and dress like other emergent church leaders. Non-emergent church leaders do the same with other non-emergent church leaders. White-collar professionals seek out white-collar professionals. Liberals look for liberals, conservatives for conservatives. NASCAR lovers look for other race car enthusiasts, and 20-somethings look for 20-somethings. This is part of what it means to be a conformist.[1]

In youth ministry, we've talked forever about conformity as "peer pressure." Adolescents become increasingly interested in their friends' tastes in music, clothes, and entertainment. But we still see their parents' fingerprints all over their choices, too. Listen to a student's response to something you're teaching, and you often get good insight into the views held at home. Many of them have conformed to their parents' likeness far more than they'd admit!

Attend many youth worker conferences, and you'll see this same conformity in action among our peers. There's the common set of jokes that usually involves senior pastors and board members, middle school students, and van breakdowns. If you try to count the number of goatees or "soul patches" on the men at these conferences, you'll quickly lose track because they're everywhere. And a few hot topics and programming agendas seem to drive the conversations of most of the youth workers in attendance. Conformity is all around us.

The youth ministry culture has jumped on the bandwagon of cross-cultural service and global activism. We celebrate that! But our concern is that your interest may subside if the youth ministry culture stops talking about global engagement. Is there something deeper behind why you'll disciple youth for global awareness and involvement?

SELF-AWARENESS

It's pretty easy to observe the socialization process of conformity among our youth and in others we encounter. It's much more difficult, however, to see it in ourselves. Yet an intentional effort to become more aware of how we've been conditioned to view the world is an essential first step toward responding to global needs. Our awareness of others' needs begins with becoming more aware of ourselves. Specifically, we need to step back and see how we've been conditioned to view particular issues and people. That's one of the things we want you to do throughout each of the following chapters. How do you feel about the topics at hand? What kinds of responses do they elicit in you? To what degree are those responses due to how you were reared? In what ways are they products of present conversations with friends and colleagues?

We all experience small episodes of this kind of self-awareness. Maybe it's when we hear ourselves say something and suddenly think, *That's my mom's expression! Nobody else I know ever says that!* Or maybe your kids spend time with your best friends and say to you afterward, "Now I know why you do *that!*" You become like the people with whom you have coffee. But are you aware of how this shapes you and your view of the world?

We want to move beyond these occasional moments of self-awareness and intentionally become aware of how we see the world. We need to notice the connection between our conditioning and how we respond to people, issues, and circumstances in our global village. Self-awareness is a very difficult thing for people to master, but especially for youth workers and perhaps most of all for veteran youth workers. The demands of youth ministry typically require continual movement, lots of energy, and limited margin for deep thinking. But here are a few ways to enhance our self-awareness as we keep up with the frenzied pace around us:

Spiritual Disciplines

Discipline yourself to spend time thinking about God, and how you relate to God and our world. Spiritual disciplines such as prayer, fasting, solitude, and meditation are some of the most powerful ways to become more aware of what's behind our responses and more aware of God. For many centuries, church fathers and mothers have used spiritual disciplines to "see what is, see who we are, and see what is happening."[2] The disciplines enable us to remove ourselves from the bombardment of constant stimulation to see what's going on within our souls and notice our surrounding environment and circumstances.

Create some space for the spiritual disciplines after a weekend retreat with your youth. Jot down the your weekend's highs and lows. When did you feel most alive? When were you most drained? If you felt irritated, what triggered that? Where did you see God? Where did you long to see God more? Of course doing this requires some intentional awareness in the midst of the retreat, but simply taking time to reflect on a weekend like this is a helpful way of going deeper. Don't just describe what happened; think about your reactions to various events, big and small.

Developing self-awareness requires discipline. It moves us away from the cycle of constant movement to a space where the Holy Spirit can help us move beyond the borders of our preconditioned responses to the needs of the world. You can also develop this awareness as you watch the news, talk with friends about current events, and go to the movies. Think about why you respond the way you do to the global "hot topics" of the day. As globalization presses in, we'll need to move beyond our own borders and think and respond as global Christians.

Short-Term Missions

Use your own short-term mission experiences to deepen your awareness. International travel is one of the leading ways to enhance global awareness. But it's also one of the primary ways to enhance *self*-awareness.[3] It doesn't happen automatically but being in different environments affords us opportunities to see our culture and ourselves in a brand-new light. The opportunities are largely dependent upon the degree to which we can interact with locals in the places we visit. Merely observing life on the surface doesn't provide a whole lot of awareness about the local context or ourselves, but when we have conversations with people who live there, a few dramatic things can occur.

1. *We often learn a way of seeing the world that differs from our own.* For example, we may discover different ways of defining success and failure or new ideas about how to respond to tragedy.
2. *We observe the world's issues and problems first-hand.* Missionaries and news channels are no longer our sole informants about what's occurring globally. We can encounter these realities up close and then be challenged with how to respond in Christlike ways.
3. *We can become more aware of how our culture shapes our pursuit of faith.* For example, if we take the time to have meaningful conversations with Christians in the communities we visit, we'll undoubtedly find many core issues and values we embrace together. But also it's likely that we'll encounter God-fearing people with very different views on issues such as speaking in tongues, the role of women, or dating versus arranged marriage. Some will see your views as too liberal, and others will see you as too conservative. Don't be fearful of these differences. They're a powerful way to learn more about who God is through Christians from different cultures and to deepen your own walk with God. So, given that short-term missions are pretty much a staple for youth ministry across the board, tap into their potential to enhance your awareness of yourself, God, and others.

Diverse Community

You don't have to travel overseas to benefit from the self-awareness that can come from being with a diverse group of people. Look for a community of friends and ministry partners who come from many backgrounds—ethnically, denominationally, politically, professionally, and more. Rather than solely spending time with people who look like you, view the world like you, and agree with you on every point, seek out people who see things differently. That doesn't mean you have to become a chameleon and conform to everyone else's ideas and opinions. In fact, interacting with a diverse community might end up reinforcing and solidifying many of your thoughts and convictions. But if we truly want to minister beyond the borders of our own subcultures, then we—like the apostle Peter in Acts 10—have to be open to the Holy Spirit leading us in new directions with renewed confidence.

Look for ways to become more aware of how you view the world. How would your faith be different if you grew up in a different home/city/country? What would your ministry look like if you came from a different ethnic background? How do your friends shape the way you see the world? What's your theology of mission based upon your personal and ministry priorities? Be intentional about how you're conditioned to view the world and its needs.

"SOUNDS TOO POLITICAL . . ."

This brings us to the next issue—politics! Most of the topics addressed in this book have political undertones. The environment, caring for the poor, and immigration are often polarizing topics that—depending on your viewpoint—can get you painted with a particular political stripe. This is especially true in the U.S. where the questions don't usually begin with ethics, stewardship, or theology but with what's a "red" versus "blue" opinion or idea. As a result, Christians often go quiet or run to one of the political corners to take sides.

But we must remember that there are committed and thoughtful Christians on each side of the political aisle. We plead with you to keep that in mind as you read this book. Don't write off a topic because it seems to belong to the "other" side of the political spectrum. We need to consider how we as Christians should engage with this issue—and especially how we should disciple our youth to do so. That's our primary concern here.

Depending on your political viewpoint, you can turn on talk radio or the cable news channel of your choice and hear and see global issues portrayed through particular perspectives. Unfortunately many of the debates polarize the conversation and do little to move us forward in response to the world's needs. Many liberals write off conservatives as uncompassionate, and many conservatives dismiss liberals as irresponsible. And meanwhile, millions of people can't afford to get medical treatment, human trafficking continues, and our fellow human beings around the world die of hunger. Slavery, genocide, and abortion all get worse when the church is silent or avoids engagement because it's too political. Name-calling, fear, and anger do little to help our fellow image-bearers living in desperate circumstances. Therefore it's time for the church to step up and offer a compelling response; fortunately, many youth ministries are leading the way.

As Christians, we must get personally involved politically, but that's not our primary interest in this book. No political party or movement gets to lay claim to any of these issues or the necessary responses anyway. Our devotion is first and foremost to God's kingdom, a counterculture organized around the benefit of the underdog. Christian engagement politically and in humanitarian issues flows from our identity in Christ as his kingdom subjects. And as youth workers, we all have the privilege of discipling our students to live as they were created to live—in a world and dominion characterized by peace, love, and justice. Our driving interest in this book is to tap into the unique resources available for meeting the world's needs through Christian youth—both today and in the years to come.

RIGHT, WRONG, OR DIFFERENT?

When I (Dave) travel with my kids, they get really sick of hearing me say, "It's not weird. It's different." Of course when they tell me about some new trend among their friends, and I respond, "That's just weird!" my girls retort, "Dad. It's not weird. It's different." *Touche!* This is quite a shift from the emphasis in my growing-up years where the primary thrust in our home was putting everyone and everything into "right" or "wrong" categories . . . and with very little room for gray. My parents' mantra was, "When in doubt, don't do it!"

This does raise a question: *Is anything right or wrong anymore*? Do we just name our perspectives and preferences about various issues and move on? Christians everywhere embrace a core set of beliefs and values. There is wide agreement among Christians worldwide about some defined categories of right versus wrong, regardless of one's upbringing and cultural conditioning. There are some universals of morality that apply regardless of culture. For example, almost all Christians see the disregard for human life as wrong, not something simply to be left up to a culture's collective interpretation and values. And Christianity is opposed to corruption and embezzlement by businesses, governments, and religions regardless of the cultural norms. We hold that it's not simply the option of a culture to determine morals. Instead, Christians believe that the morals taught and lived by Jesus supersede cultural notions of ethics.

Therefore our global engagement can't merely be a programmed outgrowth of how we've been conditioned. Our youth will see right through that. Some things are right, and some things are wrong. And there are many things in between that aren't only good or evil. So we can't quickly label our personal preferences as right versus wrong. We need to develop theological responses rooted in the hard work of studying the Scriptures together with followers of Jesus around the world, and then discern in community how they apply to the pressing issues of our day.[4]

Theologian Richard Cunningham offers some encouragement (and caution) in this regard:

> Our challenge is always to remain open to a new word from God or a new breeze of the Holy Spirit without being enticed by every siren's song that catches our ears. Throughout the universal church, we must learn how to say "no" as well as how to say "yes" to local theologies and how to achieve the wisdom to know when to do which.[5]

Diverse views among Christians are not a problem to be solved. They're the blessing of God! They allow us to see more of God's infinite, beautiful character. But in the midst of our diversity, we must remain united that Jesus is the Way, the Truth, and the Life. "If we fail to stand fast here, everything else will be in vain and the Christian church will lose its bearings. We will fail in our missional vocation to be the image of God and the body of Christ in the world."[6]

FINAL THOUGHTS

Expect to feel a variety of responses as you read about the issues we've included. Those reactions don't come from a vacuum. They're connected to your deeply rooted ideas and assumptions about how the world should work and the role of Christians therein. When you feel energized and compelled toward an issue and idea, pay attention to that. When you feel uncertain, skeptical, or numb, pay attention to that as well. This kind of reflection will improve how you help your youth encounter these issues because they're all going to feel a variety of responses as well.

We have to move beyond responses that are primarily a result of our conditioning. We (Dave and Terry), too, have some differences between us on the politics of these issues. It's made for some good dialogues while writing this book. But we're 100 percent united in agreeing that our reason for getting involved with these issues is first and foremost because God made us for this. Understanding and engaging with the world not only allows us to be more fully human, but it's also part of how God designed us—to reflect God's image by caring for one another and the world we share. Moreover, we were created to live out the image of God together in community with the rest of humanity—something we can now do on a global scale unlike ever before.

But in order to live out our humanity, we all need to see the big picture, understand how our world is connected, and appreciate its diversity and complexity. In so doing, we have the chance to respond to extreme poverty, corrupt regimes, and pandemics such as HIV-AIDS and malaria. We have unprecedented opportunities for living out the presence of Jesus on the planet. And as we prepare our students to understand the increasingly interdependent world they will inherit, we offer them a profound opportunity to serve with us as its stewards.[7]

What can we do? Recognize the people who have shaped your view and continue to do so. Then enter into the next part of the book with an enhanced awareness of how you've been conditioned to respond. Keep an open heart to how the Spirit wants to direct you.

PART 2
LEARN

Having spent some time bringing focus to our wide-angled perspective, it's time to zoom in on several specific issues facing our global village. While the issues we've included aren't exhaustive, we have selected seminal global concerns that should be addressed in our youth ministries. Any one of these issues could easily merit an entire book, but we want to give you a summary of each topic with some tangible ways to respond.

Each chapter begins with a case study that has value for both you and your students. Feel free to reproduce these for use in your ministry. All of the case studies are based upon real situations we've encountered, but some of the details have been changed to respect the privacy of the individuals involved. After the case study, you'll read some background on the issue, including a description of the topic and some related history and statistics. And every chapter concludes with several practical ways you can help your youth respond to this issue, along with additional resources for more information.

What can we do? *Learn* with us what it means to disciple youth so they can be followers of Jesus in our 21st-century world.

CHAPTER 3

"ME? RICH? YEAH, RIGHT!"

POVERTY AND HUNGER

CASE STUDY

The youth group from Sandy Creek Church in Cleveland, Ohio, had just returned from a 10-day mission trip to Bolivia. The team of 18 high school students and four adult leaders stayed and worked in a rural community of indigenous people and helped build a new medical clinic. Jake, a high school junior, was one of the students on the trip. His first morning home, Jake's mom asked him to pick up a few things from the grocery store.

Getting behind the wheel was bittersweet for Jake. It was great to be able to drive again, yet he couldn't help but picture the family he'd stayed with—they had no car; they walked everywhere. They'd never even been to La Paz, a city just an hour's drive from their home. As Jake drove by the neatly manicured lawns in his neighborhood, he was struck by how clean everything looked. But why did he feel so uncomfortable, almost nauseous? He passed a little girl riding her bike and wanted to yell, "Hey! Do you know how good you have it?!" Turning on the radio was no help; the deejay was complaining about having to work on such a beautiful summer day. *Whoa! Rough life, man!*

When Jake got to the grocery store, he headed straight for the bread aisle. Nearly an entire aisle was devoted to different kinds of bread. He stared at all the choices, and his eyes welled up with tears. Suddenly he wanted nothing more than to sit down for breakfast with his host family for *salteñas*—a pastry filled with meat and potatoes that they'd served him on his last morning.

Jake's youth leader had said that his host family probably sacrificed a lot to feed him that kind of meal—and here he was, back in the U.S., spending a $50 bill his mom handed him for "a few things" for the day. Jake's host family wouldn't see that much money anytime soon.

After he arrived home the night before, Jake explained to his own family that 70 percent of the people in Bolivia live in poverty, and the indigenous people in the village where his group had stayed are among the poorest and most discriminated-against people in the country.[1] Jake told them about the two-room house where he'd stayed, the thatched-roof church in the village, the water well shared by several families, and how much he wished he could go back for the whole summer next year. His mom's face glowed with pride as Jake talked while his younger sister mumbled, "Well, aren't you the next Mother Teresa?!" Jake's dad said, "There are lots of poor people here in Cleveland, too, Jake—especially because all our jobs keep getting sent to people in countries like that."

Jake couldn't really expect them to relate. But it made him feel lonely, distant, and annoyed. He wanted to go back to the simplicity of life in Bolivia. He didn't want to just return to life in the suburbs and forget about the previous 10 days.

Jake drove home from the grocery store in silence, replaying the dinner conversation, his experience at the grocery store, and endless images in his mind from the last 10 days. As he walked in the door, his mom said, "Hey honey—what do you think about doing your back-to-school shopping today?"

Questions for Further Reflection and Discussion

- What is your initial reaction to this story? Do you relate to Jake or feel annoyed by him? Why?
- How have you, or others you know, had similar experiences?
- What do you observe about Jake and his family?
- How might Jake channel his encounter with poverty?

High school students and youth workers aren't exactly living the high life—right? Doctors, lawyers, professional athletes—*they're* the ones with summer homes and exotic vacations. The rest of us are just trying to get by. But check out *http://globalrichlist.com* and see how we fare on a global scale. A teacher earning $50,000 is among the top 1 percent of the highest earners—the richest people—in the world. The top 1 percent! So, what if someone makes barely $20,000 a year? That person is still among the top 11 percent of worldwide moneymakers. And for high school students working 20 hours a week at minimum wage, they're easily in the top 15 percent of the richest people in the world. That's right—a high schooler working a part-time job makes more money than 85 percent of the people in the world. The disparity between these levels of income and spending validates some of the angst Jake was feeling after 10 days in Bolivia.

However, if Jake is like most of us, the pressures and demands of being thrust back into the North American lifestyle will cause his high-minded thoughts about poverty to quickly dissolve. Studies show that even a few days back inside the social machine of consumerism and materialism will make it difficult for him to sustain his heartfelt desire to think and live differently for the sake of people like his new Bolivian friends.

This is a chapter about poverty. We briefly encountered some of the economic realities of our global village in chapter 1. In this chapter, we need to more fully understand poverty and its implications for our work with youth, then consider some ways to respond.

POVERTY: AN OVERVIEW

What does it mean to be poor? *Poverty* means lacking the basic necessities of life. *Poverty* means hunger. It means lacking clothes and shelter. It means being sick due to preventable illnesses and not being able to get medical help. *Poverty* means being unable to obtain safe drinking water. It means living one day at a time, having no access to school, not knowing how to read, and not being able to get a job. *Ultimately, poverty is powerlessness to change your situation.*

Reread that last sentence and understand what poverty means. *People in poverty have almost no chance of getting out of their circumstances.*

Ministering to the poor takes time, and that's why most of us avoid the responsibility of ministering to them. But lest the poor and their troubles seem like "distractions" from our primary focus in youth ministry, many authors in Scripture have a different take on the poor and God's expectations for his people. The following are just a few:

- Give generously to [the poor] and do so without a grudging heart. (Deuteronomy 15:10)
- Rich and poor have this in common: The LORD is the Maker of them all. (Proverbs 22:2)
- The righteous care about justice for the poor, but the wicked have no such concern. (Proverbs 29:7)
- "When the Son of Man comes in his glory, and all the angels with him, he will sit on his glorious throne. All the nations will be gathered before him, and he will separate the people one from another as a shepherd separates the sheep from the goats. He will put the sheep on his right and the goats on his left . . .
- "Then he will say to those on his left, 'Depart from me, you who are cursed, into the eternal fire prepared for the devil and his angels. For I was hungry and you gave me nothing to eat, I was thirsty and you gave me nothing to drink, I was a stranger and you did not invite me in, I needed clothes and you did not clothe me, I was sick and in prison and you did not look after me.'

  "They also will answer, 'Lord, when did we see you hungry or thirsty or a stranger or needing clothes or sick or in prison, and did not help you?'

  "He will reply, 'Truly I tell you, whatever you did not do for one of the least of these, you did not do for me.' Then they will go away to eternal punishment, but the righteous to eternal life." (Matthew 25:31-33; 41-46)
- Suppose a brother or sister is without clothes and daily food. If one of you says to them, "Go in peace; keep warm and well fed," but does

nothing about their physical needs, what good is it? In the same way, faith by itself, if it is not accompanied by action, is dead. (James 2:15-17)

- If anyone has material possessions and sees a brother or sister in need but has no pity on them, how can the love of God be in that person? Dear children, let us not love with words or speech but with actions and in truth. (1 John 3:17-18)

Of all the experiences on short-term mission trips, the encounters with deep poverty are probably the most significant. However, the long-term impact of those significant encounters isn't clear.[2] It's even possible that without intentional follow-through, the long-term effect of short-term mission trips can be *greater materialism* rather than increased sacrifice and stewardship.

While many of our fellow image-bearers struggle to survive, many of us pursue middle-class lifestyles (that are more upper class when you consider the extras). What we once considered luxuries now seem like materialistic "rights." It's easy to spend $200 per month just to be "connected"—cell phones, satellite TVs, high-speed Internet, GPS devices, and monitored security systems. We might feel as though we deserve daily lattes, luxury appliances, big (really *big*) screen televisions, home theaters, matching and fashionable furniture, new cars, big houses, and ever-expensive visits to sporting events, concerts, and other creature comforts.

While we're conditioned to strive for these luxuries, we're often unaware of the growing divide between the haves and the have-nots. Many of the poor are getting poorer, unable to access some of the basics, let alone dream about any of the wealth those "on the other side of town" enjoy. It's easy to grow comfortable knowing that the poor are remaining poor, even in our own communities. Check out these numbers:

- In the U.S., the top 20 percent of earners make 50 percent of the total income nationwide. The average annual income among this group is $132,131, with the top 5 percent earning far more.
- The bottom 20 percent of earners make 4 percent of the total income in the U.S.[3] Their average annual income is $18,116.[4]

But only 48 percent of U.S. citizens see their country as divided along economic lines.[5] Every American community contains whole subcultures of poverty, invisible to those who don't live around it or who have shrugged it off while quoting the Bible (out of context), *The poor we will always have with us*. When people in poverty want to move into our middle-class communities, most of us adopt a "not in my backyard" philosophy and work to keep them at a distance.[6] And if we charted the amount of time most youth ministries spend addressing poverty, many would get very low marks.

Poverty has many faces across the globe. But the call to action remains the same—a call to serve the world so that many more of our fellow human beings have enough to eat, adequate shelter, access to education and health, protection from violence, and a voice in what happens in their lives and communities.[7]

To be fair, people in many parts of the world are doing better than in previous generations. Global life expectancy is at an all-time high. Just 100 years ago, life expectancy was merely age 41 *in the U.S.*—a lot of us reading these words (including the ones who wrote them!) would have been long dead. But the life expectancy of people worldwide is now 66—and much longer in the developed world. Per capita incomes are on the rise, and global hunger is in mild retreat. Why? There are many reasons for the progress in these areas, but the biggest cause is that people like us are doing something about global injustice.[8]

Roughly 5 billion of the world's 6.8 billion people are making progress on most of the scales used in the developed world, which include metrics such as life span, literacy, health, and freedom. But more than 1 billion people are still trapped in circumstances that seem more befitting the 14th century—civil war, plague, early death, and squalid living conditions. Most of these countries are concentrated in Africa and Central Asia with a few scattered elsewhere. As countries such as China, India, Brazil, and Senegal race toward new levels of success, countries such as Chad, Burundi, Haiti, Laos, North Korea, and Uzbekistan are heading toward what might be called the black hole.[9] There are under-resourced people in every nation of the world, but there's a heightened level of desperation among these 1 billion people.

Whether it's the poorest 1 billion or the homeless in Sao Paulo or Cleveland, the disparity between the haves and the have-nots is appalling. As we've pointed out, most people in the world are poor—and by global standards, most of us reading these words are rich by comparison. Poverty is a complex topic that development experts spend their lives researching and understanding. But many questions remain: *To what degree is poverty a result of poor governments, bad policies, lazy people, and inadequate natural resources? How about globalization, war, and exploitive religious movements*?

All of these issues are partly why so many of our fellow human beings continue to live in poverty. And while overly simplistic and utopian campaigns to end poverty aren't helpful, we can all still do something. We're all called to use our minds and our hands to make the planet a place that raises the dignity and value of all people—a big task that begins by making sure everybody has the basic resources to survive.

So let us move forward to the next step of understanding and responding to global poverty.

WHAT CAN WE DO?

The rising awareness of our increasingly connected world calls us to think creatively about the inequality between the haves and the have-nots. These are grave matters of moral significance. And while you and your students can't end poverty, you certainly are capable of doing whatever you can with your modest resources to make a difference in the lives of our fellow human beings.

An important note: We believe the best hope for Haiti, Burundi, and Laos lies in Haiti, Burundi, and Laos. This is a theme you'll hear from us over and over throughout these chapters. In other words, people in the developing world have already demonstrated that they can accomplish more for their own communities than outsiders—and their grandiose plans—can. But there are some tangible differences we Westerners can make alongside them. Here are a few ways to get started:

Give

Youth groups have shown amazing abilities to raise money for mission trips, camps, and amusement park adventures. Why not try putting some of that fundraising energy into helping a particular group of people? The Sandy Creek group that traveled to Bolivia could continue to raise funds to help meet some of the needs of the people they encountered on their trip. Sometimes as little as $35 can provide the funds needed to help a family start a business (see *kiva.org* for an easy way to do this). Or a student like Jake could challenge his peers to give up two sodas and, in turn, use $2 to buy a Lifestraw—a complete water purification kit that provides clean water for a year.[10] One local agency is challenging adults to give one hour's wages each month to help the poor. Everyone could do that!

Consider structuring your tithing toward making sure people have indispensables—vaccines, antibiotics, food supplements, as well as better seeds, fertilizer, roads, water pipes, textbooks, and medical personnel. In his book *The White Man's Burden*, economist, William Easterly notes, "This is not making the poor dependent on handouts; it is giving the poorest people the health, nutrition, education, and other inputs that raise the payoff to their own efforts to better their lives."[11] Do your homework to find out how to ensure that your money gets to the poor and helps meet their real needs.

Start a Subversive Movement

Students can be challenged to subtly weave the topic of poverty and hunger into many of the contexts where they already find themselves. Are they stumped for topics for the "informative speech" they have to give next week or the paper they have to write? Encourage them to research and report about the plight of the poor. Direct them toward statistics and real stories of people who live from one meal to the next. Encourage them to show the human face of poverty. Equip students to creatively bring up the topic in conversations with friends, family members, and in classroom conversations. Challenge them to include it in their Facebook posts. Encourage the artists in your group to weave it into their songs and paintings. Have some of the writers compose poems and articles for their school newspapers. Inspire those with part-time jobs to talk to their employers about campaigns for the poor.

Others in your group might want to start a Web site that links to information on the poor and provides stories of what your group is doing about it. Maybe your group can sponsor an event for your church, school, or community that creates awareness of global poverty and allows people to make their own contributions to help the poor. Or you can challenge your students (and yourself) to consider how important that new outfit really is, and how they can instead use their purchasing power to respond to the inequities between the haves and the have-nots. Raise the voice of the poor by infecting the conversations of your group with stories, statistics, and challenges regarding the dire circumstances facing the majority of the people in the world. Put a face and voice to the poor among those in your reach.

Advocacy

Encourage your students to expand your subversive movement beyond their own circle of friends and family to media leaders and government officials. Put pressure on local and national media outlets to publish news and feature stories on the poor. And begin by instilling in students the importance of exercising their voices as citizens. Even though most of them haven't reached voting age, they will soon. How does what your group is learning about the poor affect the choices being made by local, state, and federal governments?

It's easy to believe that one more letter of petition or phone call won't make much of a difference; but despite the many foibles of government, politicians pay attention when enough of their constituents raise a stink. "If we can make enough noise and demonstrate that there will be a cost for those politicians who just ignore us, then we can change things . . . This is the foundation of the democratic system. Either use it, or we lose it on the issues we care about most."[12]

Interact with the Poor—Up Close

There's some truth to what Jake's dad said—that there are poor people in Cleveland, too. Nearly every community has people living in poverty (albeit with very different conditions than what the world's bottom billion wage earners experience). But sometimes we need to see the reality of poverty right in front of us, especially if we're secluded in more financially well-off parts of our community. For a wake-up call, go together to under-resourced neighborhoods in your area. If at all possible, work with a local church or agency that's already doing work there as opposed to blowing in uninvited. You don't necessarily have to bring money or food—though that's not a bad idea. Instead, talk to people and learn about their living conditions.

And look for opportunities—personally and with your students—to interact with the poor as you go about your other tasks. When a homeless person in the city approaches you, resist perpetuating the homeless-people-just-want-money-for-more-booze myth. Take time to stop and talk to people who ask for money. Look them in the eyes. Listen to their stories. Invite them to have a meal with your group. It's inspiring to help people who are in need in Bolivia or Haiti, but we do have a responsibility for showing love and respect to the poor in our own neighborhoods.

Vocational Counseling

Students desperately need mentors and leaders who can help them discover how their deepest longings and concerns intersect with the world's needs. They need voices that guide them toward meaningful vocations. Some of your students might be future researchers who can discover ways to improve the support systems. Others might be future aid workers or missionaries who gain expertise in local settings and bring about tangible change that addresses poverty in local communities. Still others might be future business people who outsource differently after having interacted with the raw realities of poverty. Some might be future pastors who will provide supernatural perspectives to the issues of poverty and hunger. And most of them will be parents who have a deep influence on their own families. Therefore begin planting the seeds to help students think about investing their work in something that matters. My (Dave) book, *What Can I Do?: Making a Global Difference Right Where You Are*, deals specifically with this topic of orienting work, whatever the profession, around global issues.

FINAL THOUGHTS

There are many other ways your group can tangibly respond to the crisis of global poverty. It's likely your best ideas will come from having your group brainstorm together on how to respond to encounters with the poverty of much of the world. The options for responding to global poverty are abundant, from fun Web sites such as *www.freerice.com* that allow you to simultaneously improve your vocabulary and fight world hunger to YouTube contests with groups such as the United Nations World Food Program. Why not pick a few useful ones for your group and go for it?

Most youth and the adults working with them aren't flush with money. And the pressures of surviving the 21st-century economy are very real. Our interest in this chapter hasn't been to give one more shame-filled treatise on how rich you are. Instead we've wanted to take an honest look at one of the most pressing issues of our day—the poverty and resulting hunger that exists for many of our fellow human beings.

So let's stop seeing the poor as problems to be solved and rather as individuals to be loved; let's stop viewing them as "victims" and instead help them discover their talents and ways to sustain their lives. And let's break the habit of feeling guilty when thinking and talking about the poor and discover that together we can make a difference.

RESOURCES

The Gospel of Luke

The End of Poverty: Economic Possibilities for Our Time by Jeffrey Sachs (2006, Penguin)

The White Man's Burden by William Easterly (2006, Penguin)
A Framework for Understanding Poverty by Ruby K. Payne (2005, aha Process, Inc.)
Poverty Facts and Stats (http://www.globalissues.org/article/26/poverty-facts-and-stats)
ONE Campaign (http://www.one.org)
Micah Challenge (http://www.micahchallenge.us)
One Life Revolution (http://www.30hourfamine.org)

CHAPTER 4

SILENT KILLERS

HIV/AIDS, MALARIA, TB

CASE STUDY

Samuel, a 13-year-old orphan living on the streets of Zimbabwe, has AIDS. He doesn't really know what that means except his brother died of it and one time he heard a missionary say, "AIDS is God's punishment." Evidently, God has lots of punishing to do in Samuel's family. Samuel's mother died, too—in her case it was malaria. After she was gone, Samuel stayed in a shelter for a while. But when the workers learned he was HIV-positive, they secluded him from everyone for fear he would infect others and always wore gloves before touching him.

Convinced he'd be better off on his own, Samuel escaped from the shelter to live on the streets. Every day he wondered if it might be his last, but what did it matter? There was no real future for him anyway. Each day consisted of trying to steal enough food to survive a little longer. When he wasn't scavenging for food, he sniffed glue—a cheap escape from his emotional and physical torment.[1] Samuel knew the "remedy" was bad for him, but at least it numbed the pain.

Samuel hung out with other street kids, but he never told them he was HIV-positive. He felt sick most of the time and had a chronic cough and fever. Some days he ran into groups of visitors from the United States (a.k.a. short-term mission teams) who fed him great meals or gave him a new shirt and shoes. They told him about God and his love. They wanted him to say a prayer that would ensure he'd go to heaven. But Samuel wasn't too sure he wanted to spend eternity with a God who punished his family with afflictions such as malaria and AIDS. Nevertheless, he usually said the prayer because it made the visitors so happy. Then, the visitors would always leave after just a few days.

Questions for Further Reflection and Discussion

- How should short-term mission teams relate to people like Samuel? What does the gospel look like for street kids like these?
- What issues contribute to the problem of HIV and other pandemics?
- How can we address the issues of God and his love when so many individuals experience something so different?

For most North American teenagers, sickness is a minor inconvenience (with the side benefit of missing a day or two of school). Malaria is something we make sure to avoid by taking a few pills before a short-term mission trip, and tuberculosis (TB) sounds like something people caught on the *Titanic*. Most of us have heard plenty about AIDS, but surprisingly most North Americans don't know someone in the U.S. living with this growing pandemic. From many North Americans' perspectives, AIDS happens to homosexual people, adulterers, drug addicts, and people in Africa. It's a faceless disease to most of us.

Silent killers, including HIV/AIDS, malaria, and TB are not everyday realities for most of us, but they are for many communities around the world. There are cures for malaria and tuberculosis, but these medical cures are unavailable to many of our fellow human beings. There are growing numbers of prevention programs and treatments for HIV/AIDS, but again, they're out of reach to many around the world who most desperately need them.

In this chapter, we want to explore several issues, including the scope of the problem of disease, consider prevention versus treatment programs, and think about the unique nature of a Christian response. Then we'll end with some specific suggestions for how we can respond.

THE SCOPE OF THE PROBLEM

Nearly a half billion people get malaria every year, and 1 to 3 million of them die because of it. Most of the victims are young kids. Ninety percent of malaria-related deaths occur in Sub-Saharan Africa. Malaria is both a result and cause of poverty. It's part of a vicious cycle in our fallen world (Genesis 3:19).

Almost a third of the world's population has been infected with TB. It's transmitted through the air, and someone's infected with it every second. Between 1 and 2 million people die of TB each year, too. It's the leading cause of death among adults, killing more worldwide than all other infectious diseases combined.

Then there's HIV/AIDS. The number of people living with this disease is at an all-time high. More than 40 million people have it, and 1.8 million contracted the disease this year. In Sub-Saharan Africa, HIV/AIDS is the leading cause of death and accounts for 76 percent of the global HIV/AIDS toll.[2] The stories coming out of places like Mozambique, South Africa, and Zimbabwe are devastating. In the Western world, HIV/AIDS isn't near the death sentence that it is in other places. Consider the likes of former NBA star Magic Johnson who's been living with the disease for more than 20 years.

There are way too many boys like Jean-Paul, a skinny Rwandan kid who is HIV-positive. Jean-Paul has a very large skull, and he cries all the time. He says, "People are laughing at me because I have a big head and a skinny body. A doctor gives me drugs; I don't know what they are for, but I take them anyway." [3] He hopes the virus is going away, but everyone seems to keep their distance for fear they'll catch Jean-Paul's "curse."

More than half the world's HIV-positive people live in Sub-Saharan Africa. But that means there are still 20 million people living with it elsewhere. About 1 million Americans are infected, a quarter of whom don't even know it.[4] The World Health Organization (WHO) warns that Russia, India, and China could face an HIV/AIDS pandemic that trumps the one in Africa. In fact, the WHO reports that if present trends continue, China will have the highest levels of HIV/AIDS per capita of any country in the world by 2015. Many factors contribute to this reality, including increased drug and sex traffic, cultural resistance to speak openly about sex, and an overly simplified "condoms-only" approach to the problem.

Similar situations are occurring in India, Russia, and in many parts of Central Asia and Latin America. There are large numbers of individuals infected with HIV/AIDS who have no idea they have the disease. And malaria, TB, and HIV/AIDS work in tandem. People with malaria are more susceptible to TB and HIV/AIDS. For example, many in China's minority population are dying from a largely ignored onslaught of TB right alongside family members who are wilting away due to HIV/AIDS, and they pass these diseases back and forth to each other.

Zhu, a Chinese man, felt as though he instantly became subhuman when he was diagnosed with HIV. His family and friends freaked out and made sure he used different dishes from the rest of them. He, like young Samuel in Zimbabwe, left home and self-medicated by using heroin. He figures either way he'll die, whether through heroin use or AIDS. He might as well feel good in the process.[5]

With all the appropriate momentum occurring behind responses to the HIV/AIDS atrocity, it's important to remember that 2.5 as many Africans die from other *preventable* diseases as they do from HIV/AIDS. In other words, malaria and TB—but also measles, respiratory infections, diarrhea, the flu, and others. In 2002, 15.6 million Africans died from these kinds of maladies. Imagine that—far more people than populate the entire city of New York are wiped out annually from *preventable* diseases.[6]

We've only scratched the surface in exploring the enormity of these pandemics, but we aren't without hope. And while youth workers may not become disease experts, a brief understanding of the problem and some grasp of appropriate responses can help us to think effectively about what we should do in response.

PREVENTION OVER TREATMENT

Caring for the sick and diseased would seem like the only appropriate response, right? Surely there's something redemptive about supporting efforts to care for the diseased and dying. You won't hear us downplaying the appropriateness of treating sick people, but tragically some development experts point out that, for example, the compassionate initiatives to treat AIDS victims may be costing more lives than it saves. As we discuss diseases like these with students and others in our church, we're wise to look for ways to participate in *preventative* measures for responding to these kinds of diseases, not just treatment of those already infected.

Throughout most of the first decade of the 21st century, the U.S. increased funding for HIV/AIDS initiatives around the world—but it cut money for children's health care and other global priorities by nearly $100 million.[7] We don't want to reduce this to pure economics, but granting life through the *prevention* of AIDS, malaria, and TB costs far less than treating people with those illnesses. Economist William Easterly writes, "For the same money spent giving one more year of life to an AIDS patient, you could give 75 to 1,500 years of additional life . . . to the rest of the population through AIDS prevention."[8]

Again, getting into all the intricacies of how to treat and prevent disease certainly goes beyond the payload of youth ministry. However, as you get involved in short-term mission trips that encounter these diseases or partner with organizations involved in responding to these pandemics, it's important to have at least enough understanding to inform questions you might ask of groups with whom you partner.

It's always easy to find negative examples, but let's look at a more hopeful case study—the significant *decline* of AIDS in Uganda over the last 20 years. In 1988, Uganda was named the epicenter of the AIDS crisis—26 percent of the adult population was infected with it. That was the highest-known percentage of any country in the world at that point. It was impossible to keep up with treating the sick. The percentages of infected and dying people were growing, and without a drastic intervention, the entire nation would be annihilated.

Government officials, researchers, and charitable organizations put their heads together to come up with a solution for the pandemic threatening to annihilate Uganda. They developed a values-based prevention program widely known today as the ABC approach to HIV/AIDS:

A = Abstinence (from sex outside of marriage).

B = Be faithful (to your spouse).

C = Condoms (when all else failed or when people decided they "couldn't" be faithful).[9]

A and B were elevated and taught as the most viable ways of preventing HIV/AIDS for both single and married adults. But a condom distribution program was also developed knowing that some citizens would shrug off abstinence and monogamous sex as unrealistic. What happened? Uganda moved from being the epicenter of AIDS in 1988 to being the least infected country in Sub-Saharan Africa today. Here are the numbers:

- In 1988, 26 percent of Ugandan adults were HIV/AIDS positive.
- In 2003, 4 percent of Ugandan adults were HIV/AIDS positive.

In 2003, several nongovernmental organizations advocated moving toward a more broad-based approach to HIV/AIDS treatment in Uganda. They believed that teaching abstinence and faithfulness was antiquated and unrealistic, and the government agreed to move toward a "C" only approach—distributing condoms. The result? By 2008 the infection rate in Uganda had doubled—climbing from 4 percent to 8 percent.[10]

How do we get at stopping the causes of pandemics like HIV/AIDS, malaria, and TB in the first place? That's the question we've been interested in raising in this section. With a glimpse into some of these issues, we're better prepared to consider what we can do to respond in our own ministries.

THE CHRISTIAN RESPONSE

Lots of businesses, schools, and nonprofit organizations share a concern about the silent killers devastating so many people in our world. But what, if anything, is unique about how we should respond as Christians and youth ministries? Initially, many Christians viewed HIV/AIDS as God's punishment for sin: A consequence of bad choices (sexual promiscuity, illicit drug use, etc.). We've moved beyond that interpretation in most contexts, but the Christian response is still varied—from fears of not knowing how to explain why God allows these atrocities and apathy and silence about TB and malaria to discrepancies between care and treatment for AIDS victims in Miami compared with AIDS victims in South Africa.

When the WHO reported that China's HIV/AIDS issue would trump the pandemic in Sub-Saharan Africa, the Chinese government took note and recently reported that the number of HIV/AIDS cases is increasing at a rate of 53 percent each year in China.[11] The Chinese got busy and consulted the Ugandan government to learn more about what it did to reverse the HIV/AIDS numbers there. Ugandan officials shared their use of the ABC prevention approach, and their Chinese counterparts asked how they rolled out the program and educated people from urban centers to remote villages.

Here's how: The Ugandans tapped into the most grassroots organization throughout the country—Christian churches. They exist in every city, town, and village. The churches learned the program and became educational centers for teaching the ABC approach based upon the Bible. Although Chinese officials haven't always welcomed the presence of Christian churches throughout their country, they understood the validity of what their

Ugandan peers were saying and began working with some Chinese churches to respond to HIV/AIDS.

Consistent with all of history, God has an unusual ability to thwart evil schemes for redemptive purposes. Devastating circumstances and diseases are an opportunity to live out the transforming power of the gospel.

WHAT CAN WE DO?

How can one person or youth group realistically make a difference? Well, for instance, you and your students might be the ones who hold the hands of grieving TB orphans . . . or one of your students could be the one who discovers an inexpensive medicine that eliminates malaria once and for all. Both now and in the future, there are various ways we can disciple students to respond to global pandemics.

Pray

Prayer is often eclipsed by more "practical things." It seems easier to place our confidence in going somewhere to do something, giving money to a group, or writing a letter to a congressperson to increase funding for preventative treatments. These are all things we encourage you to consider. But confidence in God's supernatural power is central.

Consider committing to a weekly time when your group will pray for those suffering from disease. Or fast one day per month as an entry point for your group to begin praying for specific people dealing with these issues. Organize prayer bands within your church to get others praying with you. Check out the Ecumenical Advocacy Alliance for a great resource on reflection and prayer (http://e-alliance.ch/en/s/hivaids/resources).

Create Awareness

Start by briefing your youth about these diseases—or better yet, get a few of them to do it. Many students care deeply about these issues, so tap into their passion and get them some tools to help them teach the rest of the youth group and church. Then look at ways you can be an educational resource to your community at large.

Teaching sessions that challenge negative attitudes and uneducated responses about those infected are a good start—but look at other ways to create awareness and teach about these things, too. You could organize an AIDS walk in town. Or make good movies and Web sites available. Or encourage students to write editorials for your local newspaper. Or get the attention of local TV stations. Or host a sporting event fundraiser like those promoted by Grassroot Soccer (www.grassrootsoccer.org). And as always, it never hurts to get your group members brainstorming ways they can be a voice for the voiceless and diseased.

Organize an Art Expo

Especially if many of your students possess artistic abilities, they can use their art to give the faceless a face. Find humanizing ways to get painters to paint respectful pictures of people with TB and malaria. Get filmmakers involved in creating awareness through documentaries or short vignettes. Poets, musicians, sculptors, and graphic artists can all be encouraged to orient some of their artistic expression to creatively engage people infected by silent killers by making them less silent and more visible.

Vocational Counseling

It's important to help your students see how responding to silent killers might be part of their vocational pursuits. What future scientists will invent new preventative measures? Who are the future health care workers who can compassionately be living responses to these issues? How can artists, poets, teachers, businesspeople, and preachers use their platforms to increase awareness and redeem this evil?

Let's Talk about Sex

Don't ignore the obvious relevance of HIV/AIDS to your own students' sex lives. Much of the attention on HIV/AIDS in youth groups is focused upon innocent women and children in Africa suffering from AIDS, but it's also a silent killer in your town, church, and youth group. And STDs continue their prevalence among youth domestically. Therefore, straight talk about sex is a no-brainer. Don't shy away from it.

Link with Other Churches and Organizations

None of us can single-handedly solve the issue of pandemics or save an entire generation of orphaned children. However, your ministry can have a significant impact on an individual, a local church, or a village. Many churches and youth groups are already responding to this issue, so begin by finding out what's already being done.

Partner with specific churches, ministries, or youth groups in specific places to fight silent killers. Intersect with this issue up close. Make an effort to send multiple groups to the same villages each year, stay in contact with the people you've met, and build a long-lasting relationship with them. It's amazing the impact on both communities when long-term relationships are forged.

Then work together to develop a plan of health education and preventative tactics to help reduce the contraction of diseases. In other words, instead of devising a plan and taking it to the village, have your youth group work with the village to find a plan that is effective *and* culturally sensitive.

Consider teaming up with an organization to provide clean drinking water systems to villages. Diseases like malaria spread through contaminated water and kill thousands each year. You can reduce many of these problems with simple drinking systems that can be installed in villages. Check out some of these organizations:

- Bless China International: www.blesschina.org
- World Relief: www.worldrelief.org
- Blessings International: www.blessing.org
- Water Aid: www.wateraidamerica.org

FINAL THOUGHTS

Turning a mosquito bite into a fatal bout of malaria is a symptom of our corrupt, fallen world. So are the devastating effects of TB, HIV/AIDS, and many other infections. But God is reversing the curse of evil—and often doing so through students like yours. Many teenagers in churches around the world have a fire in their bellies to do something about this issue. Many governments that have previously resisted any involvement from Christian churches are reacting to their despair over the HIV/AIDS crisis by welcoming churches' help in reversing the curse of AIDS.

Join the growing number of churches and youth ministries living out Christ's love to eliminate silent killers. The fight begins by turning up the volume on these killers and invading them with knowledge, passion, creative skill, and prayer.

RESOURCES

Black Death: AIDS in Africa by Susan Hunter (New York: Macmillan, 2003).

Breaking the Conspiracy of Silence: Christian Churches and the Global AIDS Crisis by Donald E. Messer (Minneapolis, MN: Fortress Press, 2004).

The Hope Factor: Engaging the Church in the HIV/AIDS Crisis by Tetsunao Yamamori (Federal Way, WA: Authentic & World Vision, 2004).

Disease Statistics (http://www.cdc.gov)

The Ecumenical AIDS Advocacy Alliance (http://www.e-alliance.ch/en/s/hivaids)

Grassroots Soccer to fight AIDS (http://www.grassrootsoccer.org)

Unite for Children against AIDS (http://www.uniteforchildren.org)

Videos on African diseases (http://africaresource.org/index.htm)

CHAPTER 5

SEX AND SOLDIERS FOR SALE

HUMAN TRAFFICKING

CASE STUDY

Alek desperately wanted his parents to stay together. But despite his hopes and prayers, they divorced two years ago. On top of the pain of seeing his family ripped apart, divorced families in Albania are often treated like outcasts. Alek and his mom, Elira, recently moved across the border to the bustling metropolis of Athens, Greece. While some find the ancient/modern world of Athens inspiring, Alek hated being there.

Soon after Alek and his mom were settled, Elira fell in love with a guy named Nick. It was hard for Alek to be excited for his mom because Nick treated Alek like dirt. Pretty soon Alek and Elira moved in with Nick. The longer they stayed in Athens, the less Alek saw his mother. She was sleeping when he left for school and gone by the time he got home. She was rarely home before he cried himself to sleep at night. What kind of mother leaves her son on his own to deal with a new country, new school, and new father?

Little did Alek know that his mother was fighting for his life and hers. It turned out that Elira's new "lover" expected her to sell her body as a way to pay the rent. When she resisted, Nick threatened to kill her and Alek. Nick took as payment any money she earned from turning tricks. When Elira didn't have much to hand over, Nick beat her.

One night Elira woke up Alek and they escaped to a nearby hotel. She reported her pimp to the authorities, and he was eventually prosecuted. At last she was free. But the problem remained—she couldn't find other work. So she continued to offer men sex for money in order to survive. Of course, Elira didn't tell Alek what her job was. She told him she worked at a tavern, but he figured it out. He wished his mom would just tell him the truth. Most nights she came home bruised, sad, and distant.

Meanwhile Alek longingly watched boys his age walking with their parents through the park across the street. He wondered what it would be like to live a "normal" life like them. More than anything, he wished he and his mother could just move back to Albania where he'd no longer have to be an outsider, and his mother would no longer have to sell her body.

Questions for Further Reflection and Discussion

- Alek comes to you for advice. What would you recommend?
- To what degree do you believe prostitution goes on in our own community?
- How should your church respond to a situation like this?

We learned about slavery as kids in school—southern plantation owners abusing, buying, and selling people to turn a profit. Thank God we've moved beyond that barbaric era . . . right?

Not so fast. Elira, the Albanian woman in this chapter's case study, is a 21st-century slave. She didn't come from Africa to pick cotton, but when she arrived vulnerably in Athens, what she thought was a budding romance turned into an abusive master-slave relationship. For Elira, slavery means being molested weekly by hundreds of strangers and enduring violent rape, sometimes multiple times a day.

Or meet James, a nine-year-old boy from the Democratic Republic of

Congo who was forced to be a soldier. Slavery for him means sleeping with a gun under his head, being forced to kill people, performing sex acts with other soldiers, and knowing he may die of starvation.

Slavery didn't end in the Civil War era. In fact, there are more people enslaved today than during four centuries of the trans-Atlantic slave trade.[1] There are more slaves today than ever before.

A SNAPSHOT OF HUMAN TRAFFICKING

Human trafficking is an international crisis that includes people like Elira who are forced into prostitution, and people like James who are forced to kill. People are trafficked for a variety of other jobs, including domestic help, construction, and farming. Elira and James are among millions of people trafficked annually.[2] And not just in faraway places such as Greece and the Congo, either; it also happens in North American cities such as Albuquerque and Toronto and on farms in Alabama and Michigan.

Human Trafficking Facts

- It's estimated there are 13 to 27 million slaves worldwide, with an additional 1 million added each year.
- Most slaves are women and children.
- Trafficking has no socioeconomic bias—it happens in the wealthiest neighborhoods in the United States and in the slums of India.
- Human trafficking is estimated to be a $32 billion industry, exceeding the annual profits of Starbucks, Google, and Nike combined.

Women and children are the largest group of victims, most of whom are caught in an endless cycle of indebtedness that's nearly impossible to pay off. For example, women such as Elira are told they owe a $75,000 debt, usually due to an exorbitant price put on their lodging, food, clothes, etc. And no matter how many times a day they sell their bodies, trick after trick, they can never make enough money to pay off the debt. In fact, their debt grows faster than their earnings.

Thousands of child soldiers like James are forced to fight in armed conflicts around the world, especially in places such as Myanmar, Sudan, and Congo. As you can imagine, many of these kids end up dead before they reach adolescence. Some choose to stay in the military, even when given the choice to leave, because they see it as their only way to survive poverty and war. And for some, being a child solider means at least they're armed to protect their families from warlords. The life of a child soldier is one of violence, abuse, disease, and an imminent risk of starvation.[3]

The sale of people is lucrative business—and the traffickers aren't the only beneficiaries. Others who profit from this barbaric business include weapons manufacturers, condom manufacturers, the person selling chocolate that came from slave labor, the taxi drivers who drive customers to brothels, and the fast-food restaurants supplying food to traffickers waiting for their "product" to be sold on a cold, dark street corner. In many situations, the local police are making a profit from this, too, by getting paid to look the other way.

We noted earlier that this crime is as close as our own backyards. Trafficked people can be found all throughout the developed world in urban, rural, and even suburban settings. Similar to the international crisis, sex trafficking is the largest U.S. form of slavery. Women and children are often unknowingly recruited into strip clubs, street-based prostitution, escort services, and massage parlors. Pimps target runaway youth or homeless kids, offering them a place to live, food to eat, "freedom" from their parents, and some income. The average age of entry into U.S. prostitution is 12 to 13 years old. The typical victims aren't just homeless youth in Miami or L.A.; they're kids from Indianapolis, eastern Colorado, and Saskatchewan. Growing numbers of U.S. traffickers are scouting for recruits at restaurants, bus terminals, traveling carnivals, peddling/begging rings, and in traveling sales crews.[4] This isn't a faraway issue. This is an industry targeting *your* students.

Toledo, Ohio, is the second largest area in the U.S. for human trafficking mainly because of its major highways running in all directions. Traffickers rotate teens among highway welcome centers, hotels, and truck stops. And because of Ohio's proximity to Detroit and its large farming areas, trafficked women, children, and even men (for slave labor) can be hidden and then used for slave labor or sex for profit.[5]

Another predominant form of trafficking at home and abroad is in the agricultural industry. Many large farms employ undocumented immigrants as seasonal farm workers, promising them a chance to gain citizenship and freedom in the U.S. But somehow the foreign farm workers never seem to do enough to "earn" their freedom. And the traffickers threaten to turn over the immigrants to authorities if they run away.

Slavery takes huge emotional, spiritual, and physical tolls on its victims. The layers of mistrust, trauma, abuse, and spiritual doubt are far beyond what victims may even be aware of. Many victims believe all hope is lost. Women like Elira sometimes separate from their traffickers but continue working in prostitution because it becomes a habit or addiction. Or they may not know how to find employment elsewhere, so they keep selling their bodies in order to support themselves and their families. Trafficked children often miss out on learning how to read and write, and the only "skill" they've learned is having sex with men. Hope and change can feel out of reach. It's not enough to simply free slaves—something more is needed.

CALLING FOR ABOLITIONISTS!

Breaking through the layers of corruption and stopping this global problem can seem impossible; but Christ, the Victor, calls us to stand up for the Eliras and Jameses of the world. Ironically, Elira's name means "freedom." As one created in God's image, Elira was meant to be free from the visible chains of prostitution, as well as the less-visible chains of guilt and fear. Even individuals who work in the sex industry by choice are enslaved and in desperate need of freedom. You know that from the stories we hear of high school girls who offer sex to guys at school to earn some money and feel accepted.

But they were made for so much more! What does it look like for the freedom of Christ to become real to people enslaved like this?

Stopping human trafficking is no doubt a fight of great resistance. The battle against the sex trade seems even more perplexing when you consider some governments have legalized prostitution, including New Zealand, Amsterdam, and the state of Nevada where legal brothels are open 24/7. The fight against all forms of human trafficking is messy and complicated, but we need to stand up—and with Christ, anything is possible.

The good news is that the fight has begun. There are hopeful stories out there, and there are organizations and individuals around the world devoted to bringing justice to the oppressed. Large organizations such as International Justice Mission operate in developing countries around the world, simply trying to help governments enforce their own legal system as a way to stop traffickers and free their victims.

Many smaller organizations focus on more specific agendas, such as freeing cocoa farmers in Cote d'Ivoire, helping victims of prostitution in

Bangkok or Chicago, or rescuing child soldiers in Myanmar. For example, Nea Zoi—a ministry devoted to helping the Eliras of Athens—has a team of workers who talk with about 100 enslaved women on the streets of Athens every week. They listen to their stories, tell them about Jesus, try to find them safe lodging, connect them with legal help, and work toward getting them training and jobs. What a powerful picture of Jesus' presence up close! Telling an Elira "we're praying for you" is a nice start, but without the willingness to do something more, it would be a bit of a crock. Several other organizations similar to Nea Zoi are surfacing around the world. You could take some time and learn about one you and your group can connect with.[6]

But while the fight has begun, the battle is far from over. The church needs to be deeply engaged with this issue rather than just waiting for the United Nations or other organizations to take care of it. The Scriptures have plenty to say about God's heart for justice and the oppressed. Therefore let's combine our proclamation of the gospel with the demonstration that Jesus' saving power applies to the issue of trafficking.

So many of the global issues we're addressing in this book are interconnected. Human trafficking is linked to problems of poverty, AIDS, domestic violence, drugs, weapons trafficking, and hunger. Awareness of this global problem of evil demands we stand up and defend the millions of victims entrapped in slavery and put a stop to those who buy and sell them.

WHAT CAN WE DO?

Many of today's students are deeply concerned about this issue, so you probably won't have to look far to find some of them to take up this cause with you. Here are a few ways to get started—but be prepared for some who may be ready to run hard at joining a new movement of abolitionists!

Education and Awareness

As with so many of the issues in this book, education and awareness are important parts of responding to this crisis. At the end of this chapter is a list of resources to assist you in this process. You'll also find stories of victims and survivors among these resources. The person saved from human trafficking could be one of your own students! And many of them might play powerful roles in making slavery a relic of the past. Inspire your students and learn together what you can do. A few ways to begin include:

- Lead a Bible study that focuses on hope or justice. Check out the *Deep Justice* materials from our friends at Fuller Youth Institute (http://fulleryouthinstitute.org).
- Ask a counselor or a local professor to speak to your students about the issues of trauma connected with trafficking.
- Show a movie or documentary on human trafficking such as *Born into Brothels* (2004). This film chronicles kids living in the red light district of Calcutta. Invite the parents of your students to join the viewing and discussion afterward.
- Raise awareness in local schools, other churches, and in your community.
- Post flyers at toll-road plazas with hotline numbers and general information about trafficking.

Some students may be affected emotionally or spiritually in ways you don't expect. Be sensitive to individual needs. Ensure these needs are addressed by having appropriate parents or adult leaders available to follow up with them.

Learn how to spot trafficking in your own community. The "Help Identify and Refer Victims" section under the Combatting Human Trafficking link on the Salvation Army Web site has a list of the identifiers (http://salvationarmyusa.org). If you live in the U.S. and suspect someone is a trafficking victim, he or she can get help regardless of immigration status (call the National Human Trafficking Resource Center hotline: 888-373-7888).[7]

Pray and Give

The familiar responses of prayer and giving can't be overstated here. A dark, demonic network has a hold over victims, traffickers, and customers in this decadent industry. Combine illicit sex, force, violence, and power, and you have a recipe for Satan's ugliest work. This is not primarily a battle against flesh and blood; it's a battle of supernatural proportions. Pray and recruit others to pray.

Also pray for those who are directly involved in ministry to trafficked people. Many of them encounter the demonic oppression of this vile industry first-hand. They need our intercession. Choose one or more of these groups with your students (from the resource list at the end of this chapter) and commit to pray for them on a regular basis. Contact the group and ask about its specific prayer needs. Don't underestimate the dual role this will play for them—the power of prayer and the encouragement it offers during such emotionally draining work.

These groups always can use financial gifts, so consider creative ways to contribute to one or more of these groups with your wallet. Some suggestions:

- Challenge your students to give up paid entertainment for two months and use that money to pay for meals for victims who've been freed from their traffickers and are living in safe houses.
- Combine raising awareness and funds by hosting a youth-sponsored dinner for your community. A portion of the amount you charge for the dinner can go to cover the costs of a ministry's street outreach to women forced into the sex trade. During the dinner students can share information they've learned about trafficking and the specific group receiving the gifts. Ask students to think creatively about how they want to share information. Some ideas may be: writing a song about a victim's story, expressing the emotions of this evil through a painting or drawing, or creating a wall of photographs taken by students to exhibit what freedom means to them. This not only benefits the respective organization but also creates awareness of this global atrocity.

Advocate

Trafficking victims don't have access to the resources we take for granted. They may be held under lock and key and may not even know their exact locations. In addition to physical barriers, many are held in prisons of fear due to threats of violence. These women, children, and men need others to advocate for them—and as Christians, it's our responsibility to advocate for the oppressed.

Young people's opinions are valued more today than in the past. They have opportunities to take their voices to new levels. Therefore encourage your students to exercise their voices in society. This might take shape by raising awareness in their schools, or writing letters to their congresspersons, asking them to support laws that help victims of trafficking and bring justice to traffickers. The more we raise our voices, the better the chance someone will listen. And don't stop at a letter from just one person to a government official. Pass around a petition and send it with the letter. Challenge your students to use resources they have access to, especially social networking tools such as Facebook, to obtain as many signatures as possible while at the same time raising overall awareness. Invite a local congressperson to your youth group and ask him or her how to get the federal government to pay greater attention to this issue.

Responsible Consumerism

Victims of the labor trade have made some of the goods sold in our stores. How many times have you bought chocolate this year? Who harvested the cocoa beans in that chocolate? You might not have a clue, but with a little research you can learn whether the chocolate you enjoy was made on the backs of slaves. More than 35 percent of the world's chocolate is made from cocoa beans grown in Cote D'Ivoire where children are forced to work all day long.[8] Check out http://stopthetraffik.org for more information on whether or not your chocolate is "slave-free."

Enlist a few students to do some homework on products to avoid. The Fair Trade Federation has information on responsible buying on its Web site, as well as a tool to locate stores in your area that sell fair-trade products (http://fairtradefederation.org). Encourage students to take the information home and discuss a buying plan with their parents, teachers, and peers. Your local community could help starve the traffickers by making it repulsive to buy trafficked items! The more households that commit to purchasing fair-trade products, the closer we get to ending forced labor. Your students are capable of starting a movement in their own backyards. It really can be that easy.

Offer Dignity and Respect

When talking about victims of human trafficking—whether they're working in prostitution, laboring in a field, or carrying weapons in their young hands—these victims are people. They're God's creation. Throughout your education and conversations with students, encourage language that removes derogatory terms from the "job" a person is being forced to perform—such as "the prostitute" or "hooker"—and instead refer to them as "victims of prostitution," etc. Watching our speech is a good way to start treating these individuals with the dignity and respect they're due as fellow image-bearers of God.

FINAL THOUGHTS

There isn't a fairy-tale ending to the lives of Elira and Alek—at least not yet. Elira is still working the streets of Athens, but with the help of some local

Christians, she's going to school and plans to start a business. Sometimes she goes to these friends for prayer and encouragement, and at other times she keeps her distance. Alek is old enough to join a youth group any day now. He's still just a kid, but he's witnessed more X-rated kinds of realities than most adults. Alek is encountering some good Christians in Athens who show him Jesus by the way they help him with homework and talk to him about life with Jesus. He needs peers who care about his life and the trap in which he and his mother live. Their story is not uncommon. But as more of Alek's peers become aware, pray, give, buy responsibly, and advocate for him and his mother, there's more reason to hope.

The topic of human trafficking is *en vogue* right now, but that's not why we're into it. We have to stand up for the women, children, and men who suffer the effects of slavery. We can—and we need to. Let's revolt against this evil and enlist our students to join others in freeing all the Eliras and Aleks.

RESOURCES

Born into Brothels documentary (Image/Thinkfilms, 2004—note: Rated R).
Music by Emmanuel Jal about life as a child soldier in Sudan (www.emmanueljal.org)
End Slavery Now (www.endslaverynow.com)
Fair Trade Federation (www.fairtradefederation.org)
International Christian Alliance on Prostitution (www.icapglobal.org)
International Justice Mission (www.ijm.org)
Invisible Children (www.invisiblechildren.com)
Polaris Project (www.polarisproject.org)
Stop the Traffik (www.stopthetraffik.org)
U.S. Department of State; Annual Trafficking in Persons Report (www.humantrafficking.org/organizations/427 or www.state.gov/g/tip/rls/tiprpt/2008)

CHAPTER 6

TECHNO-CRAZINESS

TECHNOLOGY AND MEDIA

CASE STUDY

Kenneth grabbed his backpack and headed for the door. The long school day was over. As he pushed open the door, Kenneth flipped on his cell phone. His school recently clamped down on cell phone use because some kids were caught cheating with them. A lot of his friends still text at lunchtime, and Kenneth has done so secretly from his locker.

Kenneth was looking forward to a laid-back Thursday night. Two of his favorite TV shows would be on soon. He'd head home, check Facebook, and then do his homework before the shows started. As he hopped on the bus, he noticed 17 text messages on his cell, about half as many as he would send by the time his 15-minute bus ride was over. He needed to coordinate the weekend's activities, which included playing some *Guitar Hero* with his friend and watching a movie with the guys. Saturday was soccer practice, and his parents had already warned him they had a list of chores for him.

His mom got home from the office about the same time as Kenneth. He hopped on the family's desktop, and his mom fired up her laptop. Just then his younger sister Sheila came in the front door. She didn't respond to his "Hey Sheila" (although she was lip-syncing to music on her iPod). Shelia went into the family room to play a video game before doing her homework. She liked to play multiplayer with her school friends, a benefit of wireless Internet in the house.

As Kenneth checked his Facebook page, he returned a few text messages to finalize his weekend plans. His mom just "poked" him from her laptop and Kenneth rolled his eyes. He visited a few of his teachers' Web sites to see what homework he needed to do while simultaneously responding to a couple of instant messages that popped onscreen. He also downloaded a new song, browsed headlines on the CNN site, and did some work (while six instant message windows remained open on his computer screen). He started doing some research on Google for a paper he needed to complete for English class, pasted some quotes into Word, and picked up his cell to see who was calling.

Questions for Further Discussion and Reflection

- To what degree does this mirror your life?
- What issues does this raise for you? Are there any subtle reasons to be concerned about this family?
- What do you see as the greatest opportunities for technology and youth ministry? What are the greatest challenges?

The story of Kenneth and his family could be set in any major city of the world. From Sao Paulo and Mumbai to Oslo or Seoul, the world of technology has surrounded our lives, and the youth of the world have happily grown up in its embrace.

Whenever most observers write about youth and technology, they make a few common mistakes. The first is supplying an enormous number of statistics to support their claims—because a year later, those statistics are out of date, technology has changed, and the underlying issues get lost in the numbers. Do you really care about how many teens use Facebook or listen to satellite radio? The members of today's young generation are "digital natives"—they've grown up with keyboards of various shapes and sizes. But at some point these too may become obsolete, and then Kenneth and Sheila will reminisce, "Can you believe we once had to type our school papers?"

The second mistake is to focus on youth without comparing their technology patterns to adults'. The world's fascination and preoccupation with youth has forced some to talk about media and youth in ways that are either blatantly inaccurate or aren't any more significant than, or different from, the technology habits of their parents.

So in this chapter we describe some global technological trends, examine the underlying issues, and list some practical implications for youth ministry. We want to pull back the curtain a bit and help you understand how globalization, technology, and youth intersect.

TECHNOLOGICAL TRENDS

For years, no one had a firm grasp on what was going on with global youth and technology. Yahoo and OMD conducted one of the first global research projects, the results of which are reported in *Truly, Madly, Deeply Engaged.*[1]

In 2009 two more studies emerged: Nielsen surveyed youth from 50 countries and debunked some popular myths about teens' media usage. They concluded, "Taken on whole, teens exhibit media habits that are more similar to the total population than not."[2]

MTV, Nickelodeon, and Microsoft interviewed 18,000 kids in 16 countries and discovered youth love technology because it keeps them connected, usually with friends they already have. The study found numerous similarities among teens around the world but with some regional differences.[3] For example, Japanese young people prefer mobile phones while Chinese youth spend the most time on the Internet of any national group. Northern Europeans watch the most television while teens in countries with "outdoor" cultures (e.g., Italy, Brazil, and Australia) rely more on mobile phones.

So what global trends are emerging that will impact our youth over the next decade? Whatever emerges, it's safe to say that technology will play a central role in shaping youth and their existence. Here are a few key threads worth watching:

Not a Substitute for the Real Thing

As the Internet exploded and adolescents ran to social media sites such as Myspace and Xanga, youth experts began to explore "virtual identity"—the way teenagers pretend to be someone quite different in the online world. Though there are instances of this practice, research has shown that, for most teenagers, technology is not a substitute for the real thing. Rather it's an extension of their social worlds.[4] They use the Internet to engage in "friendship-driven" practices. Some friends include people they've never met and who may live in other countries; *but the vast majority of teens use technology to be in constant contact with their friends.*

Mobile Devices

Cell phones are the medium of choice for the majority of adolescents. Mobile devices represent the platform expected to gain the most momentum over the next 10 years. Like Kenneth in our case study, many teenagers are on the computer just minutes a day, usually to check Facebook or do homework. The connectedness with others comes via the cell phone. While some youth around the world have been relying on their hand phones for years, the U.S. cell phone market has traditionally been more oriented toward business clientele. That's changing. In 2004, 45 percent of U.S. teenagers owned a cell phone; in 2009, 75 percent did.[5] The biggest jump for cell phone ownership is age 14, the age when most American teenagers start high school. Surprisingly, research suggests that most teens still use landline phones for the majority of their phone conversations, reserving texting for their cell phones. This trend also seems to be changing.

Easy Come, Easy Go

Youth possess little loyalty to particular forms of media. It's all about what keeps them most connected to their peer group, and what their parents allow. Adolescents often jump into new technology not fully aware that it's not as innocent as it seems. As pedophiles patrolled Myspace blogs, parents and their kids flocked to the "safer" Facebook. Expect to see continued shifts in their media loyalty.

Big Brother Is Watching

As mobile devices grow in their power and capabilities, the trend is leaning toward greater interaction between GPS-enabled mapping systems and the person using the cell phone. While this makes teens' whereabouts known 24/7—their parents can track them minute by minute—youth seem unfazed. Some companies are more than unfazed; they're developing targeted marketing efforts that will send sales alerts and texts messages to cell phone users as they walk by various businesses.

Online Broadcasting

The ability to create your own audio and video content and post it online is growing exponentially. The growth is likely to surge dramatically now that it can be done from mobile devices such as cell phones, MP3 players, and tablets. Hulu, YouTube, Pandora Radio, and NetFlix gained prominence and efficiency just within the last five years via online broadcasting. Imagine what will happen over the next decade . . .

So, pay attention to the technological trends evident among your students. Look for ways to use technology to address global realities and beware of the subtle but ubiquitous power of technology near and far.

THE UNDERLYING ISSUES

Because of the Internet, the enthusiasm for movies, books, and trends moves across cultures quicker than ever before. And yet underneath is the perpetuation of Western ideas such as individualism, consumerism, and even friends with benefits. There are a few underlying issues with technology that we need to continue to watch. They include:

How We Think

Much research demonstrates the way media and technology shape how the brain functions. This isn't a new phenomenon. The printing press moved most people away from getting their information primarily through listening and toward getting it through reading. Today the first instinct for many of us looking for information is to go to the source of all knowledge—Google! But the instant answers we usually get from Google alter the way we think and process information.

Children ages two to five spend an average of 25 hours a week watching TV and another 7 hours a week with DVDs or TiVo. Psychologists say the result is a wandering attention span. Youth have learned to value and pay extra for immediate information, exchange, and interaction. In short, our willingness (and even ability) to wait has disappeared.

The Internet's use of text promotes quick soundbyte thinking, which often works against a thought process that wrestles with dissonant ideas or considers things deeply. It's no wonder attention spans continue to drop as we move from 22-minute television shows to two-second status updates and 140-character posts. One University of London study found that individuals who are constantly connected via email, texting, and social networking sites experienced a 10-point drop on an IQ test. In fact, researchers found that constantly being "on" via technology has a similar effect to regularly giving up one night of sleep. The problem isn't using those forms of technology but the constant distraction that occurs from the pings of emails and texts.[6]

What We Think

Technology also shapes what we think. In chapter 1 we note Jennifer Gidley's hypothesis that media and corporations have colonized youth's imaginations. Fashions, trends, and ideas spread with an unprecedented speed from one side of the world to the other due to technological advances. There are some inherent dangers to this. Gidley writes, "Since the advent of television, and video game parlors, followed by the use of computer games . . . Western children and youth have been consistently and exponentially exposed to violent images . . . The imagination, like the intellect, needs appropriate content to develop in a healthy manner."[7]

There's also a positive power that exists in the way technology exposes youth to new ideas. The Internet allows a free exchange of ideas where grassroots movements can communicate and present their messages. This free exchange has opened new doors for authors and musicians once limited by the control of large corporations. Youth ministry needs to place a strong degree of energy into discipling students to think, listen, view, and use technology with discernment and intentionality. Rather than just mindlessly using and consuming, teenagers need to be taught how to use technology with eyes wide open.

Identity

In our world of technology, youth are willing to share personal information with people they've never met in person—data their grandparents may have been hesitant to provide to a next-door neighbor. Today's adolescents consider it normal for personal and financial information to be stored online, in servers thousands of miles away. As youth extend their social networks online, they're seamlessly woven into various Web sites. The regular practice of posting pictures and videos of themselves online reveals a comfort with giving up a level of control to technology.

Living out one's identity in a virtual world is also what's behind sexting—using cell phones to send and receive sexually explicit photos and text messages. The anonymity or distance created by technology often leads adolescents to online behavior they'd never think of doing in person. About 15 percent of teens have sent sexually suggestive content—text messages, emails, photos, videos. But before we get too carried away, realize that more than 30 percent of adults have sent suggestive photos of themselves to other adults.[8]

WHAT CAN WE DO?

In short: Use technology.

Maximize text messages, social networking, and Web sites to communicate with your students, foster midweek interaction, and reach out beyond the borders of your youth room. Remember that email is old school for most teenagers, but they live with cell phones in their hands—therefore use text messaging and Facebook.

But bear in mind that there's no substitute for the real thing. If we had to jump up and down about something here, it would be this point. Nothing we do via technology, particularly online contact, is a substitute for face-to-face time. Youth ministry, at its core, is still a life-on-life process when Christian adults take intentional steps to enter the lives of teenagers and serve as fellow travelers along the journey with Christ. So, for example, don't send email as an entry point to a conflict-laden situation; instead encourage your fellow youth workers to prioritize personal, face-to-face contact with students. Put down your phone and give your full attention to whoever is in front of you. With that in mind, the following are a few ways you could consider using technology in youth ministry—as well as ways you can respond to its power:

Amp Up Visuals

We live and minister in a digital age that requires some savvy use of visuals. We need to ask ourselves, *How much is too much? Is less more? Do we really need a video*? Ask your students and have them help you do this. Pictures say a thousand words, and your use of visuals says a lot about your message. Therefore don't dump a bunch of text on your PowerPoint slides. Students are really bored with text-heavy slides filled with bullet points. Instead find ways to creatively—and visually—communicate your message to your techno-savvy crowd. The technological world has forced this issue.

Prep Your Teaching

Technology has raised the stakes, and our students have grown up in an information-rich world. Nothing but the best content and teaching will do anymore. Too often our lack of study and preparation leave youth wanting. And now your teaching is stacked up against the abundance of information available to teens at their fingertips. So keep in mind that when you're ranting and raving about something, they can fact-check you faster than you can close in prayer. Technology is educating our youth, and we need to own the responsibility to teach with passion and excellence.

Moderation and Discernment

Be sure you use the power of technology rather than becoming its slave. Although many students like Kenneth can instant message, do homework, listen to music, and surf the Internet simultaneously, the brain can't focus well with that many tasks going on. Teach them when to shut off their techno-gadgets. Ask students to put down their phones when you're teaching. Use a no-earbuds policy on trips. And teach all this by example. In other words, your primary role as a youth leader isn't to respond to email. Limit the number of times per day that you check it. Show your students you can "ignore" phone calls when you're with them, and that you know how to put down the BlackBerry or iPhone in order to be fully present. Then go for a walk or run outdoors without being wired—just listen to the natural sounds for a while.

One-Week Media Fast

Challenge your group to go for a week without any technological support. Some of them would rather fast from food for a week! It will be painful. The point isn't to suggest that technology is evil. But going without it for a week can enhance their (and our!) awareness of how distracting and consuming our gadgets can be. Of course, be sure to join them in this.

Support Parents

A 2006 Pew Research study found that 92 percent of parents had rules for Internet and computer use for their teens, and 81 percent of that group had rules regarding time allowed online each day and acceptable content to access.[9] The young people you lead are not yours; they're the responsibility of their parents. That said, you must make sure your media use is in line with what parents desire. You don't want a student going home and telling mom he got to play *Modern Warfare 2* and watch an R-rated movie at the youth leader's house.

FINAL THOUGHTS

By the way, Kenneth from our case study lives in Nairobi. He's a technologically connected high school student who's proficient in English. But that's not to say all Kenyan youth are technologically connected—just as not all American youth are, either. Technology is one of the resources that further accentuates the division between the haves and have-nots. While Kenneth plays *Guitar Hero*, lives on his cell phone, and connects with Facebook friends, his peer in a nearby neighborhood carries the family's daily water supply on his head every morning. But even these water-carrying teenagers are more likely to have cell phones today than ever before.

Mobile phone use is growing fastest in emerging economies such as Kenya and India, and youth are the number-one adopters. Many Kenyan youth receive money transfers on their phones from family members living abroad. Kidnappings in Columbia are being foiled because youth are immediately contacting family and police when abductions occur.[10]

Technology can be a tremendous tool for good and for evil. We need to wield its power for good while keeping our eyes open to the potential dangers. As globalization pushes the world toward greater technological interdependence, youth who learn the skills to navigate in that world will have more power and freedom to determine their futures than those who don't. Let your students teach you about the latest trends and come alongside them to be sure they control their gadgets—not vice versa.

RESOURCES

Flickering Pixels: How Technology Shapes Your Faith by Shane Hipps (Grand Rapids, MI: Zondervan, 2009).

Technopoly: The Surrender of Culture to Technology by Neil Postman (New York: Vintage, 1993).

The Medium is the Massage: An Inventory of Effects by Marshall McLuhan and Quentin Fiore (Hardwired, 1996).

CHAPTER 7

"HUG A TREE?!"

CARING FOR THE ENVIRONMENT

CASE STUDY

Jill just completed her first semester of college. Being a Christian freshman at a state school was harder than she'd imagined. Just as she expected, some people partied constantly, but she didn't feel much of a tug to join that scene. The far greater challenge was what she faced in the classroom. Take her "Freshman Issues" class, for example. She knew it'd be interesting when she noticed that Al Gore's *An Inconvenient Truth* was required reading for the course. Growing up, the only time Jill remembered global warming mentioned was as the butt of jokes. Environmental issues were never discussed at church. As for home? Her dad came into her bedroom one snowy morning and said, "Well honey, no need to get up. It's a snow day. So much for global warming!" and walked out laughing.

But as she read through the research on climate change, it seemed like a convincing argument. She wasn't sure she bought all the abysmal despair used to motivate people, but somehow, deep inside of her, she felt as though caring about the environment was an important issue. Her professor told gripping stories about how people in places such as Cambodia and Liberia were suffering the effects of our lifestyle of consumption. On top of that, her friends were all about "going green." They even freaked out when she tossed her plastic water bottle into the wastebasket. (Of course, these were the same underage friends she helped when, after drinking way too much beer, puked half the night at the dorm. So they certainly could pick and choose the ethical issues that mattered to them.) Soon Jill was describing herself as a "green activist."

Her first day of winter break, she asked her parents why they don't recycle. Her mom said, "Oh Jill, I know we probably should, but I think the recycled stuff just ends up in the same landfill anyway. That's what Sandy told me."

During Jill's first Sunday back at church, it felt invigorating to be worshiping again with her church family. She hadn't found a church she really liked at school yet. It was so great to hear her pastor preach, too. Then he made the comment, "The world would have you believe that saving whales is more important than saving people from hell." All of a sudden she felt numb. *Does it have to be one or the other*? she thought. *Can't we care for the environment* and *share Jesus with people*?

Maybe Jill was just being an idealistic college freshman. Maybe she was being corrupted by the agendas of a secular university. Or maybe God was opening her eyes through individuals who didn't necessarily give any thought to God. She felt caught between her growing concern for the environment and the opinions of many of her Christian mentors.

Questions for Further Reflection and Discussion

- What is your initial reaction to this story?
- How would you rate how much the people in your church care for the environment?

  1 – Not very much

  2 – Most recycle their stuff

  3 – Many try to conserve and stay informed

  4 – We have some activists in our midst

- What do you think Jill should do with the dissonance she feels?

Imagine escaping to one of the remote tropical islands that sits between the coast of California and Hawaii. These islands are one of the few places left on the planet that remain almost untouched and uninhabited. It sounds like the perfect oasis after a January filled with weekend retreats, board meetings, and caring for students. No sooner are you settled into your oasis than you spot some unidentified objects floating in the ocean. Your hosts tell you it's probably from the "Eastern Garbage Patch."

It's real. In the middle of the Pacific Ocean lies a garbage patch twice the size of Texas. The garbage includes 80,000 pairs of Nike sneakers, thousands and thousands of rubber duckies that have been bobbing there since a cargo spill in 1992, a boatload of hockey equipment, all mashed together with plastic bottles, six-pack holders, and tons—yes, *tons*—of other trash. It's a convergence of international products including whiskey bottles from Japan, pill bottles from India, detergent containers from Korea, and oil cartons from Guatemala.[1]

Of all the issues covered in this book, the environment is one that most of us won't have to spend much time motivating students to care about. Several studies demonstrate that one of the greatest global concerns on the minds of youth is saving the planet—specifically caring for the environment and global warming.[2] This might be an area in which our youth can *lead* the rest of the church—to live as we were created to live, as caretakers of God's creation. In this chapter we'll examine the relevance of "green" issues to youth ministry, examine some of the most important environmental concerns, and consider several practical ways to respond to the groans of our planet.

WHY GREEN?

It's an embarrassment that Christians have spent so much time mocking environmentalists, making it more about politics than about stewardship. Granted, there is a great deal of controversy on both sides, but from the very beginning of time, we were created to care for the earth. Adam and Eve were made in the image of God, and a central part of that role is caring for the earth that God made (Genesis 1-2). Paul says Christ reconciled all things to himself, whether on earth or in heaven (Colossians 1:15-17, 20). Christ's redemption was cosmic in scope, extending to the very ends of creation; therefore caring for the earth is part of what we were created to do.

Some will rightly push back, "But isn't care for people more important than care for whales?" We have no problem agreeing with that. Surely humanity is the pinnacle of God's creation. When faced with saving a human life versus an animal's life, humanity takes precedence. But any time God's creatures are in distress, whether they're our neighbors, particular animals, or complex ecosystems, God cares. And we're God's agents of care.

Furthermore, life within our ecosystem is interconnected; therefore caring for the environment is directly connected to caring for our fellow human beings near and far. In his novel *The Hungry Tide*, Amitav Ghosh writes, "Suppose we . . . [decide] that no other species matters except ourselves. What'll be left then? . . . And do you think it'll stop at that? Once we decide we can kill off other species, it'll be people next . . . people who're poor and unnoticed."[3] Throughout this chapter, we'll continue to see the interconnectedness of planet life, whether that life consists of plants, water, animals, or people.

Over the last few years, the message of environmental responsibility has hit mainstream. It was reported that the most used word in 2008 was *green*.[4] But the idea of men and women caring for creation is as old as dirt, literally. We're both nature's rulers and servants. We're summoned to admire the beauties of creation, discover its secrets, and explore its resources. At the same time, we must conserve natural resources and make the best possible use of them—caring for God's world as God does. Therefore, on God's behalf, we're to prevent the erosion of soil, the greedy destruction of forests, the irresponsible use of energy, and the pollution of rivers, lakes, and the atmosphere. This all contributes to our primary calling to reflect God's beautiful glory in the earth God created.[5]

Six billion tons of trash end up in the sea every year, and most comes from land. You don't have to go to that remote island in the Pacific to see the results. Walk along any beach in the world and you'll find bottles, lighters, plastic bags, toothbrushes—the list keeps going. Most of this gets washed out to sea where 90 percent of planet life lives. Worldwide, nearly 1 billion people rely on fish for daily food protein. When we pollute the water, we pollute the fish. When we pollute the fish, we put at risk our fellow image-bearers on the other side of the world.

Being green is not some political or commercial agenda we ought to dismiss as a passing trend. Caring for the earth is core to how we were created to live. Discipling youth to live their best possible lives includes equipping and mobilizing them for stewardship of God's creation.

OVERVIEW OF ENVIRONMENTAL CONCERNS

There's an abundance of material available about what it means to care for God's creation. It's easy to get lost in it all, but effectively discipling youth today requires that we prepare them to live out their God-given invitation to care for creation. The following are four key environmental concerns worthy of our attention in youth ministry: climate change, energy, waste, and water.

Climate Change

Say "global warming" among your friends and colleagues, and it's likely to elicit some pretty emotional responses; some will argue it's much ado about nothing, and others are convinced the North Pole will be tropical in a matter of years. Scientists continue to research and debate the ins and outs of global warming. There's wide agreement among world leaders and scientists that humanity is producing unhealthy levels of emissions into the atmosphere.

Many of our activities distort and accelerate the natural process of greenhouse gas production by creating more greenhouse gases in the atmosphere than are necessary to keep the planet at an ideal temperature. Greenhouse gases are essential for life on earth, but this is an issue of *too* much of a good thing. Three of the most common causes behind the growing disequilibrium in the atmosphere are:

- Transportation: Carbon dioxide is produced when oil and gas are burned to run our trains, planes, and automobiles.
- Deforestation: Trees consume carbon dioxide and produce the oxygen we need to survive. They help create the optimal eco-balance God intended.
- Population growth: More people will need more food, as well as more fossil fuels for heat, transportation, and manufacturing—thereby producing more greenhouse gases.

The debate over global warming and its effects on weather and the climate continues. Supporting scientists, however, don't argue that climate change means less snow and cold for the north. Instead the predominant arguments relate to a *growing imbalance in the atmosphere* that means potentially serious consequences for humanity.

We (Dave and Terry) don't believe global warming and climate change are certainties, but there is credible science that requires we pay attention to what's going on. Prevailing theories must be continually tested against evidence and then refined; then more evidence must be collected and theories tested again. But we're wise to pay attention to the serious threat of global warming upon all of God's creation. Let's not be afraid to continue to probe the science on this and discuss it with our students.

Energy

As growing numbers of people around the world become dependent upon natural resources (e.g., oil and coal) to fuel their lives, a shortage is inevitable without innovative developments. Fossil fuels such as oil and coal are becoming increasingly rare and expensive. And of course the energy crisis is directly connected to the climate change issues we just discussed, given the carbon emissions produced from energy consumption.

There are some exciting developments taking place to move people and goods that don't require fossil fuels. And there are already new, more-affordable ways to grow food and heat homes. We need to cheer on these innovations and consider motivating some of our students to pursue careers as lead innovators in this redemptive cause. Help students with an interest in science and engineering to see that pursuing those interests with excellence and resolve can be part of how they live out their God-given mission in the world.

Energy conservation prolongs the natural resources in the earth while simultaneously reducing greenhouse gases. At the end of the chapter we'll look at some specific, easy ways to do this.

Waste

The floating island of garbage we talked about at the start of the chapter is largely a result of our throwaway lifestyle of convenience. The larger-than-Texas garbage patch adrift in the Pacific is not an anomaly. Our waterways are choked with trash. The constant push to buy more clothes, bigger homes, eat efficiently wrapped fast food, and purchase nearly disposable electronics are all connected to our problems with waste. The amount of waste we generate is shocking. Americans spend more on trash bags annually than nearly half the world spends on *all* goods.[6]

So much of our problem with waste is connected to a lifestyle of consumerism. Today, the average American produces 4.5 pounds of solid waste daily. That's three times as much as an average American produced daily in 1960, and *15 times* more waste than the average person in India produces daily.[7] Buying stuff we don't need, bringing water bottles for everyone on the road trip to the retreat, and avoiding the hassle of recycling all have an impact. Kids in Bangladesh are drinking increasingly polluted water so we can have the convenience of Styrofoam cups—except that Styrofoam won't decompose on land, and when it ends up in the water, it releases toxic chemicals. However, we can afford purified water that removes pollutants from the creation of these petroleum-based plastic cups . . . but most people in places like Bangladesh can't. Families in Brazil and Uganda are eating contaminated fish while we go on with our consumerist, ultra-convenient lifestyles. The aim isn't another mind-numbing guilt trip. But as more students and their families become aware of this issue, they can make some simple changes that can significantly reduce the problem of waste.

Water

Imagine you take 10 students on a mission trip. Eight of them get to drink safe water, but the other two have to drink contaminated water. How do you decide which two get the contaminated water? In reality, we're making this choice every day. One in five people don't have access to safe water. Pure water is in short supply. Around 5 million people die every year from poor drinking water and poor sanitation. A safe supply of water is surely an overarching environmental issue to which we must pay attention.

You'll notice that all of these environmental issues are related. Some of the reasons for limited supplies of pure water are connected to pollution from waste and greenhouse gas emissions, while other reasons are connected to our wasteful use of water. In addition, we continue to see that concern for these issues relates to both our concern for the earth God made and how we care for our fellow human beings.

The World Health Organization reports that at any time up to half the world's population has a disease associated with poor drinking water and inadequate sanitation (e.g., diarrhea or hookworm). There are some systemic issues related to this problem, some of which go beyond what we can solve from our youth groups. But as we water our lawns, enjoy long showers, or take our students to a water park, we're wise to realize there are some important ways those of us living in affluent societies can reduce the number of deaths caused by impure drinking water.

We've just touched the tip of the iceberg regarding these environmental concerns. But we want to move to a more solution-oriented way to personally and collectively live out our God-given responsibility to care for the earth and for our fellow human beings.

WHAT CAN WE DO?

We've included a laundry list of things we can do to respond to the environmental issues facing us. These aren't random acts disconnected from our calling in youth ministry; they're directly connected to our calling to equip students and their families to live as God intended us to live.[8]

Transportation

- When possible, walk, carpool, or take public transit.
- If buying or renting a car, choose one with good gas mileage.
- Frequent local restaurants and simultaneously save gas, support local businesses, and develop relationships with the servers and regular clientele.
- Slow down. You'll consume less gas and be safer.
- Keep your tires inflated to their recommended pressure to save on gas.

Energy Conservation

- Enable the sleep mode on your computer (instead of screen savers) so the monitor will deactivate after 10 minutes of nonuse.
- Plug all your electronics into power strips that can easily be switched off when you're not using them, especially if you leave home for a few days.
- Turn off the lights when you leave the room.
- Replace incandescent bulbs with compact fluorescents. (If every U.S. household replaced *one* light bulb with a compact fluorescent, it would be the equivalent of removing 1 million cars from the road).[9] Students could get creative in helping church families do this one.
- Buy Energy Star-endorsed appliances and electronics.
- Wash clothes on the cold water cycle and only run full loads.
- Turn down the heat or air conditioning when you leave the house, especially for multiple days.

- Use natural light whenever possible.
- Unplug cell phone chargers when not in use (they still use power).

Waste Reduction

- Edit on a computer screen instead of on paper. When you have to print pages, use the blank sides of documents you no longer need.
- Advertise and communicate electronically whenever you can.
- Have your students organize and manage recycling programs for your church, their workplaces, homes, or schools.
- Before buying, consider how much waste will be created from your purchase. Can the item or its packaging be reused or recycled?
- Have students sell cloth shopping bags to church members to use at the grocery store instead of paper or plastic bags.
- Use reusable cups and plates whenever possible. If you have to use disposable tableware, use paper, not foam or plastic.
- Choose simple products containing the least amount of bleaches, dyes, and fragrances and instead buy concentrated products (e.g., fruit juice, laundry detergent, and window cleaner) to reduce packaging.
- Donate and buy second-hand furniture and clothing.

Food Consumption

- Eat food that requires less energy to produce (e.g., plant-based foods as compared to animal-based) and doesn't have to travel as far to reach you (local versus imported).
- Once a week, choose a vegetarian meal when you would have otherwise chosen to eat meat.
- Eat organic food—it helps decrease the amount of pesticides used in agriculture.
- Buy (or grow!) and eat local, in-season produce. It tastes better, supports your local farmers, and requires less energy to get to you.
- Buy nonperishable items in bulk.
- Grow your own food. Or have your youth group be the catalysts to start Community Supported Agriculture (CSA) in your town. CSA connects those of us who know little about the food we eat with the farmers and land that produce it. Visit www.localharvest.org/csa for more information.

Water Conservation

- Take shorter showers.
- Turn off the faucet while brushing your teeth.
- Only wash full loads of laundry.
- Buy water-efficient toilets, washing machines, dishwashers, etc.
- Rethink how important it is to keep that lawn green.

You can easily motivate your students to brainstorm more ideas. Tap into their creativity and concern for the earth as part of how you disciple them to live their best possible lives. Demonstrate this priority by the way you recycle in the youth room, minimize unnecessary travel, and serve food at your events.

FINAL THOUGHTS

Sometimes trees have to come down, bottled water is the only realistic alternative at the moment, and printing documents is essential. However, with a few choices to take our environmental role more seriously, we can better live out our missional calling. It understandably feels as though there's little we can do to address the mammoth heap of trash in the middle of the Pacific Ocean; but by choosing to focus on even a couple of the ideas mentioned in this chapter—and encouraging our students to do the same—we can reclaim our roles as God's agents to care for all of creation.

Paul writes, "For God was pleased to have all his fullness dwell in [Jesus], and through him to reconcile to himself all things, whether things on earth or things in heaven, by making peace through his blood, shed on the cross . . . *This is the gospel that . . . has been proclaimed to every creature under heaven*" (Colossians 1:19-20, 23, emphasis added).

The gospel includes creation care.

Jesus is Lord over everything—the cosmos, the planet, the ozone layer, men and women, whales, tortoises, dogs, waterfalls, and trees. According to New Testament scholar N.T. Wright, "Preaching the gospel means announcing Jesus as Lord of the world; and, unless we are prepared to contradict ourselves with every breath we take, we cannot make that announcement without seeking to bring that lordship to bear over every aspect of the world."[10]

May our youth lead the way in being Christ's agents of redemption across the entire world.

RESOURCES

Caring for Creation in Your Own Backyard by Loren and Mary Ruth Wilkinson (Vancouver, BC: Regent College Publishing, 2001).

The Green Book: The Everyday Guide to Saving the Planet One Simple Step at a Time by Elizabeth Rogers and Thomas M. Kostigen (New York: Random House, 2007).

Serve God, Save the Planet: A Christian Call to Action by J. Matthew Sleeth, M.D. (Grand Rapids, MI: Zondervan, 2007).

Stuff: The Secret Lives of Everyday Things by John C. Ryan and Alan Thein Durning (Seattle, WA: Northwest Environment Watch, 1997).

Evangelical Environmental Network (www.creationcare.org)

Kids for Saving Earth (www.kidsforsavingearth.org)

CHAPTER 8

INVADED BY ALIENS

IMMIGRATION

CASE STUDY

Lwin, a 16-year-old Karen[1] girl, came to the U.S. from Burma 10 years ago. Her family fled Burma as refugees. There her parents worked long hours on a farm, but now they work in two different stores in Elkhart, Indiana. Living expenses take up most of their money, so Lwin helps part-time at a local Vietnamese restaurant to earn some money for clothes. Her family hasn't had to go on welfare, but some of their other refugee friends have. Lwin attends Central High School, and she recently met Jamilia, a refugee from Somalia who not long ago moved into an apartment in Lwin's building.

Jamilia (Lwin calls her "Jami") studied English in Somalia, so she's able to help her parents adjust to life in the U.S. But everything feels different here—from the way the toilet flushes, to the working elevators, to the cold winters. And nowhere does she feel more like an alien than at Central High School. Jami takes remedial classes, and most of her classmates are older guys who don't pay much attention to her. Her classmates don't give a rip about school, but Jami does. She dreams of joining students in "regular" classes. Most girls at Central look just like the pictures of American teenagers she saw online. They're nice, but they pretty much ignore her. She looks different, even from the ones with similar skin color. They act so confident and talk nonstop about who's hooking up with whom.

Jami's dream is to become a nurse. Then she could make enough money to bring her other siblings to the U.S., buy a car, and maybe take a vacation to California. If only her parents could make more money, then life wouldn't be so stressful. They already work 14 hours a day, but they are paid so little per hour. As she stares out the window, she sees four girls from the high school walking by, laughing and texting on their cell phones. Jami feels very alone in the quiet apartment. She thinks about calling Lwin, but it seems as though Lwin has been pulling away from Jami. She hasn't stopped by the apartment in a long time and seems to be avoiding Jami at school.

Questions for Further Discussion and Reflection

- Who do you know at school like Jami and Lwin? Do you think this case study sounds similar to what some of your peers face?
- What does Jami need most?
- What are three to five ways your youth ministry could help people like Lwin and Jami?

Any article or seminar that covers the topic of "Changing Adolescence" usually focuses on the same topics: The power that advertising wields over teens' minds, youth in rebellion over parental influences, adolescents' fascination with risky behaviors, and kids' struggles to develop healthy identities. We dispute some of these characterizations, but for now our interest is in a dramatic change occurring in the world of youth that's discussed less often in these contexts—migration.

At no other point in history have so many people picked up their lives in one part of the world to settle in another. Some of these families are settling in your neighborhoods. Migration affects all of us, and our youth most of all.

A trip through your community will reveal the local results of migration. Both of us (Dave and Terry) live in the Midwest, yet we take cabs driven by men from Rwanda and Ethiopia, get gas from stations managed by

Bangladeshis, eat food at Chinese restaurants owned by Chinese immigrants who employ cooks from Guatemala, and we overhear women speaking Russian in line at Target and Home Depot. A similar phenomenon is happening around the world. The dramatic movement of people continues to reshape life for humans everywhere.

Further, migration has become a permanent global phenomenon.[2] Our youth are living in the midst of this phenomenon and will be rearing families and pursuing careers as the implications of this trend play out more fully. In this chapter, we want to raise your awareness about the immigration issue to help us more intentionally engage with the "strangers and aliens" in our local communities (Hebrews 13:2). And we want to provide some tools to help you respond to this growing sociological force produced by a migratory world.

A FEW NUMBERS

Again, immigration isn't just a North American phenomenon, it's worldwide. About 191 million people in the world live outside their country of origin, up from about 155 million in 1990.[3] But 75 percent of these immigrants live in only 28 countries.[4] Most of the migration between countries is toward already crowded urban centers. About 60 percent of America's more than 33 million immigrants live in its 10 largest cities.

Los Angeles counts 5.1 million immigrants within its borders while California boasts the highest immigrant population in the country (9.1 million, nearly a fourth of the state).[5] And it's important to remember that most immigrants come to the U.S. legally; the headlines regarding illegal immigration tend to skew our perspectives.

Most who migrate are moving toward opportunities (e.g., better pay, freedom of religion, access to education) or away from problems (e.g., persecution, poor economy, bad environment). In the United States, it's difficult to overstate the role of immigration. Consider the following:

- More than 34 million foreign-born people live in the U.S.—a total that doubled in the 1990s—comprising 14 percent of the population.[6] In 2011, that number will rise to 41 million. The United States is a country of immigrants, and it continues to be. Some folks have just been in the country longer. Immigration "looks" different today than it did 50 years ago because most of the newcomers have darker skin and come from places other than Europe.

- More than 11 million immigrants are undocumented residents. Immigrants without official residency and citizenship lag behind educationally, health-wise, and economically.
- One in seven workers is an immigrant, including half of all new workers. Immigrants have the same entrepreneurial "track record" as naturalized citizens do.
- One in five children in the U.S. is an immigrant or has parents who are immigrants, a number that will rise in the next decade.
- From 1980 until 1997, the number of students who were immigrants doubled[7]; and 18.3 percent of the U.S. school population consists of foreign-born students. Immigration has accounted for the national increase in public school attendance over the last 20 years.[8]

Listen to breaking news alerts about immigration, and they're usually loaded with alarming reports about increased crimes rates and loss of jobs due to immigrants. But most of these reports are unfounded or focus upon isolated events. More typically, migration offers positive results for those who move and for those who encounter them. Correctly managed, population growth can benefit both developed and developing countries. It provides economic opportunities to young, unemployed individuals who might otherwise feel hopeless. And nations that embrace immigrants gain economically by having willing laborers who often possess a stronger entrepreneurial spirit. Countries with high levels of emigration (people leaving) can benefit because the emigrants often send money back home or return to their native countries with valuable education and work experience.[9] Many European countries would have a declining population and workforce apart from immigration. And of course the vast majority of us who live in younger nations like the U.S., Canada, and Australia are almost entirely the products of immigration.

Most immigrant families have more children than is typical in places like the U.S. and Canada, so they have increased need for public services (e.g., schools, hospitals, etc.). And many immigrants are coming from war-torn places where unrest, tragedy, and economic challenges have forced them to give up careers in exchange for relative safety. Many of these individuals have seen things that no human being should ever experience. They often come into our neighborhoods after decades of heartache and tragedy. As our communities change because more and more immigrants are moving in next door, our youth ministries have a massive opportunity to express and experience Christ's love in new ways.

IMMIGRATION DILEMMAS

When families move to new countries, it's usually a huge leap from where they "belonged" to their new lives as "aliens." Among the most demoralizing issues for immigrants are the stereotypes presumed upon them simply due to their ethnicities. My (Dave) Pakistani friend who runs a Chicago-area gas station was a medical doctor in Lahore. It makes my blood boil to watch people talk down to him all day long while he waits on them at his 7-Eleven. I have a Russian friend who was a literature professor in St. Petersburg; she now works at T.J. Maxx, a discount clothing retailer. So beware what you assume about the immigrants you meet; they might have far more education and experience than you.

Most immigrants who come to the U.S. and Canada are considered suspect simply because of their physical appearance. No longer are they individuals with names, families, and unique stories; now they're often reduced to simply "foreigners" and little else. Visit any high school in the U.S., and you'll hear mainstream students describe their peers as "that Mexican kid" or "that Asian girl." Immigrants are strangers in a foreign land whom we quickly send to the margins of our culture without ever getting to know who they are. Many Christian adults and youth perpetuate racist comments about immigrants moving in nearby. We need to help soften the harsh rhetoric about immigration and develop a heart of compassion for the aliens among us.

Religion is frequently a significant value for immigrants, more often than for those in the host culture. In fact, if it weren't for immigrants coming to the U.S. from Latin America and Africa, Christianity would be on the decline. Youth ministries and churches have a great deal to gain from newly arriving Christians. And many other immigrants come from very different faith traditions. We need to exercise hospitality in welcoming people who embrace religions such as Islam, Buddhism, and Hinduism, and find ways to enter into respectful dialogue about our faiths.

Yet many youth ministries are largely unprepared to discuss Christ with the "aliens" moving in next door. And much of what we do in youth ministry is so culturally specific that it has little hope of connecting across cultures. Worse, some of what we do is downright offensive—racially, ethnically, and otherwise. So think twice before you organize a skit with someone coming out with a so-called "Mexican" or "Chinese-American" accent. The laughs aren't worth it.

And beware: A commitment to welcoming immigrants may put you at odds with local institutions and the government. In some parts of the U.S., governmental raids on undocumented workers have forced many churches and denominations to take an official stance.[10] The potential for stricter immigration laws puts churches in a difficult spot.[11]

During a May 2008 raid of a Postville, Iowa, meat-packaging plant, migrant workers—having spotted approaching Department of Homeland Security helicopters and vehicles—took refuge with their families in local churches. The pastors and congregation members found themselves in a dilemma: The immigrants they loved had lived in their community for more than a decade without any problems. Now they faced sudden arrest and deportation and were looking to the church for assistance and protection. How should the church respond? How will you respond when you have a student whose family members have been hired illegally by a local business, and you suddenly learn the family is being deported?

The immigrants in Iowa were caught in a legal crossfire. The local clergy tried to respond appropriately, but they weren't prepared. However, when over half the public school students were absent the next day, the protest grew more passionate. Unfortunately, inaction ruled the day. Aside from political candidates making a few comments, there was a prayer vigil on the 1-year anniversary,[12] and a year after that the plant reopened under new management.[13]

Inaction, however, never solves problems. A few years later, when the state of Arizona passed strict laws against suspected illegal immigrants, churches again faced legal measures that many see as unbiblical. A diverse group of churches rose to protest the law and its potential for unfair racial profiling.[14] Again, the issue placed church leaders in a difficult spot: How to be law-abiding yet conform to commands of Scripture. This dilemma is not going away until a solution is offered.[15]

Before we conclude that deportation is what these families deserve for breaking the law, aren't the businesses that hire them responsible as well—and even *more* responsible for exploiting them? And while we're debating this issue, keep in mind that many of the missionaries we send overseas are technically undocumented immigrants working illegally in places like China, Kazakhstan, and Libya.

Churches in Texas—a state with a high percentage of both documented and undocumented immigrants—have worked to understand how to live out the gospel in light of the legal system as they seek to reach out to immigrants.[16] In fact, they've hired lawyers to help them determine legal limits regarding ministry to immigrants so they can respond with Christlike love while still honoring the law. The Catholic Church has developed a list of myths regarding immigration, each countered by substantive immigration research.[17] For example, they remind people that a large majority of immigrants are here legally and want to integrate with life here the same way our immigrant ancestors wanted to when they came to the States.

While Christians may arrive at different conclusions regarding specifics about immigration, God's Word is clear that we are to have loving concern for strangers in our midst.[18]

WHY SHOULD YOUTH MINISTRIES RESPOND?

Youth ministries might be best equipped to make a difference in this global issue. Many invest significant energy to travel cross-culturally on short-term mission trips, yet it seems little energy is spent being equally passionate for ministering cross-culturally at home. Most youth ministries appear quite homogenous. Something doesn't add up. The world is literally next door. If youth ministries aren't intentional about reaching beyond ethnic and social barriers at home, they'll end up ministering to smaller and smaller percentages of their own communities.

Immigration raises some fundamental questions for youth workers, too. What are the ethical or biblical responses to those who come to your community? How does the church respond to one who is created in the image of God yet may be in the country illegally? Do we allow mistreatment or simply ignore those living illegally in our communities? Do we stand by idly while employers abuse and mistreat immigrants (while benefitting from their work)?

The parable of the Good Samaritan models how we should respond to the alien who has been mistreated (Luke 10:29-37), and Jesus judges those who fail to welcome the stranger as they would Christ (Matthew 25:34-46). As youth ministries respond to God's call to serve him to the ends of the earth, the nations of the earth are doing a lot of the "heavy lifting," moving into our states, counties, and cities.

Might your ministry have a prophetic role in how to treat families who have immigrated to your community? How do we intersect adherence to our laws with following Christ's teaching and example in responding to the alien? A core task of every youth ministry is to practice hospitality to any young person living in our communities. Youth groups can be the ideal place for students like Lwin and Jami to assimilate with other youth. One youth ministry developed some resources to assist families with legal, medical, housing, and employment-related needs. (This is most significant for just-arriving families.) You can work with local refugee ministries to teach youth and families many of the cultural practices we take for granted—like grocery shopping, applying for jobs, using an ATM, etc.

To what degree could the Lwins and Jamis in your community have different experiences because your youth group is in town? We often compartmentalize missions as a task we do far away rather than in our own towns; therefore we must cultivate hearts for immigrants that reflect the same kind of passion we have for the people we meet on our short-term mission trips. There are several ways to get started.

WHAT CAN WE DO?

Welcome immigrant families—don't "do" ministry "to" them. People who come to new cultures don't need new sets of parents. They have goals, dreams, and a history we must honor and respect. So . . . learn their stories and cultures. Ask about their families. Step outside your comfort zone and welcome the strangers in your midst. A few specific things to do include:

Get Educated

Find an expert who understands the issues immigrants may face and have him or her teach your group about what it's like to immigrate. Tell the stories and learn about the people. Start with the Scriptures and trace the teachings about how to treat aliens. And check out the Pew Hispanic Center (www.pewhispanic.org), the Migration Policy Institute (www.migrationpolicy.org), and Christians for Comprehensive Immigration Reform (http://faithandimmigration.org).

Research Your Community

Develop a team of students who can work with an adult to learn about immigrant families in your area. How many are there? You might be surprised. Where are they from? Most likely, if one family comes from a particular country, others have followed (or will follow).

Get to Know the Immigrants in Your Community

Develop trust as you learn their names, places of origin, where they work, and their needs. If possible, have them share their stories with your group. As individuals and youth ministries build relationships with their immigrant neighbors, their biases and misconceptions begin to fade. In fact, Jenny Hwang, coauthor of *Welcoming the Stranger*, says, "We see many individuals and churches transformed by their relationship with immigrants. Oftentimes, as churches begin to befriend immigrants, they begin to understand the problems with the current immigration laws and find ways to advocate for just policies as well."[19]

Teach and Tutor English

Set up a series of classes and tutoring sessions that help with clearer communication. Immigrant kids usually rush to learn English; it's typically more difficult for the older generation to follow suit. And learn the basics of immigrants' native languages; that will demonstrate sensitivity if you learn a few greetings and basic phrases. In addition, don't confuse the inability to speak English fluently with a lack of education; many immigrants are *very* educated and sophisticated. Think of what it took for them to uproot themselves and move to your community! So don't use the tutoring as a way to "lord over" them. Imagine how you'd appear and sound while trying to learn another language and culture halfway across the globe.

Offer an Extended Family

Connections with grandparents, aunts and uncles, and cousins are really important to many immigrants. The separation from extended family is one of the biggest challenges they face. So provide a community that can serve as a surrogate "family" of sorts. Give attention to celebrating their traditional holidays, etc.

Health Care Advocacy

Health care may be the most difficult cultural adjustment—and yet the greatest need—for any immigrant. The medical system is too complex for most of us to figure out, but it's much more so for people new to the states. Plus, the health care system isn't always kind to those in need. So help them establish good health practices, particularly the children. Perhaps your church has doctors and dentists who'd be willing to assist and provide discounted (or free!) health care. If your youth ask them, it may be harder for them to turn down the request.

FINAL THOUGHTS

I (Terry) recently attended a youth group, and one of the teenagers got up to share her testimony. I wondered why they asked her to do this because it seemed like she struggled to communicate and perhaps suffered from a learning problem. However, I quickly corrected my prejudice when I learned she was a refugee who had been learning English for only a few months. I had given in to a common misconception: People using new languages for them are less intelligent (when, in fact, she was very intelligent). We must not view immigrants as inferior, rather as fellow image-bearers who seek better lives and have made great sacrifices to do so.

We expect immigration issues to intensify over the next few years. By equipping our youth to respond, we're preparing them to live out the gospel among some of the most vulnerable people. Welcome the nations into your youth room and home. Discover how you can learn and grow together.

RESOURCES

Christians at the Border: Immigration, the Church, and the Bible by M. Daniel Carroll (Grand Rapids, MI: Baker, 2008).

Immigration and Migration by Rayna Bailey (New York: Infobase Publishing, 2008).

The Next Evangelicalism: Freeing the Church from Western Cultural Captivity by Soong-Chan Rah (Downers Grove, IL: InterVarsity Press, 2009).

Welcoming the Stranger: Justice, Compassion and Truth in the Immigration Debate by Matthew Soerens and Jenny Hwang (Downers Grove, IL: InterVarsity Press, 2009).

Catholic Church on immigration reform (www.justiceforimmigrants.org).

Exodus World Service (helping churches welcome refugees) (http://e-w-s.org).

Stats about immigrants in your local community (www.hometownlocator.com).

CHAPTER 9

PRIDE AND PREJUDICE

SOCIAL CLASS

CASE STUDY

First Presbyterian is a 500-member congregation in a Virginia suburb just 30 miles outside Washington, D.C. It's known for its strong youth program. Sophia and Jenna both attended the youth group at First Pres for the first time on the same night. They didn't know each other, and both girls were nervous because they didn't know many people at the youth group. Jenna recently moved to the area with her family because her dad, a physician, joined a local pediatric practice; however, Sophia has lived in the same run-down house all her life. She's been going through a rough time at home, and one day when she told the couple she babysat for, they insisted on bringing Sophia to their church—First Presbyterian.

Both girls had a good experience on their first night at youth group, and they both continued coming for the next several weeks. Jenna fit with the in-group pretty quickly, but Sophia had a more difficult time. She recognized some of the girls from school, but she wasn't friends with them, so she wasn't sure what to say to them. And the more weeks that passed, the more awkward it felt to suddenly start talking to them.

Sophia was frustrated. She really wanted to fit in at this church and get closer to God, but it felt like she'd always be an outsider.

Jenna, however, seemed to show up in a new outfit every week. And last week she was talking about how her family was going to Florida for spring break with the pastor's family. Sophia tried to imagine what it would be like to have something more than the handful of outfits she always wore. And the farthest Sophia had ever traveled was to Virginia Beach for a long weekend with her grandparents—when she was seven. Worse yet, Sophia's dad was an alcoholic.

Sophia enviously watched Jenna fit in so easily with the youth group, while she still felt stuck on the outside. She just didn't know what to say or how to act. Yet Jenna seemed to know exactly what to do.

Six months later, Jenna was on the student worship team and never missed a youth event. Sophia came only occasionally, sat in the back, and said very little to anyone. A year later, she quit coming altogether.

Sophia recently started dating a guy named Scott. You'd think she'd know to steer clear of guys like him because Scott is just like her dad. He drinks too much, and then he gets abusive. But at least he accepts Sophia for who she is. Sometimes she thinks back to her year of going to youth group and wonders if Jenna is as happy and confident on the inside as she appears on the outside. *It just seems like Jenna has the perfect life*, Sophia thinks. Sophia isn't asking for perfect, but can't she get a little break? Can anyone help her?

Questions for Further Reflection and Discussion

- What range of responses did you have as you read this? Jot down as many as you can remember. Look over your list. Try to discern the source of those responses. Why did you react in those ways?
- What is the role of the youth group in this case study?
- What do you think *should* be the role of youth ministry for girls like Sophia and Jenna?

Middle class, upper class, lower class—these distinctions seem largely removed from most of our lives. We freely walk into businesses in North America without ever being questioned, but we readily observe social class when we travel to many developing nations where it's obvious that a certain class of people is unwelcome in many hotels, stores, and coffee shops. Even if you haven't been to India, you've probably heard or read stories about the neighborhoods, dishes, and jobs reserved for the Dalits, the lowest caste among Hindus.

We could rightfully spend this chapter looking at how social class plays out around the world. But like our case study, we want to put the spotlight on pride, power, and prejudice in our own backyards. The issue of social class is closely connected to the issues of poverty that we addressed in chapter 3, but there are some additional dynamics involved.

We want to make four bold statements:

1. Social class is a formidable barrier for youth ministry.
2. Few Western Christians talk or care about social class, and many deny its influence.
3. Consumerism is continually raising the standards for what is "normal."
4. The Gospels are filled with examples of Jesus intentionally crossing social borders.

Do a quick study of any North American youth ministry or church, and you'll find that most of the people who attend any particular church are very similar—visually and otherwise. This isn't surprising given the conformity we discussed in chapter 2. Most U.S. Christians relate primarily to those with whom they share common interests, and as a result, most churches and youth ministries reflect a relatively bland, uniform mix of people. In fact, the vast majority of our churches reflect racial segregation found in other institutions and neighborhoods, and only five percent can be described as multiethnic.[1]

Similar segregation occurs along the lines of social class. We live in particular neighborhoods, attend certain schools, shop in particular stores, and dress in certain ways—all in the name of remaining within the expectations of our social statuses. Our social classes define what we talk about—our hobbies, interests, dreams, and concerns—and it defines where we live, how we look, how we parent, and what we value. So, to what degree do the people in your neighborhood, youth ministry, and church all dress the same, like the same music, have the same political views, and enjoy the same forms of recreation?

In this chapter, we want to help you understand the worldwide realities related to social status. Similar to our case study, we want to explore why it's difficult for youth ministries and churches to let people into their circles from other classes, and then we'll provide some tools to help you lead teenagers across the social barriers in your own youth group. Join us in prayerfully considering how to move beyond the borders of social class.

THE POWER OF SOCIAL CLASS

Social status teaches us how to act and relate to one another. We can quickly spot who's "in" or "out" when they show up to our groups. Even socially awkward kids can find their way "in" if they come from higher social statuses that have taught them how to act, talk, and dress. These practices aren't formally taught, they just get picked up. If you asked a "rich" kid how he knew how to act at the country club's annual gala, he'd say he didn't even think about it, he just "knew."

As seen through Jenna and Sophia in our case study, their social classes profoundly shaped their behaviors, assumptions, expectations, and overall orientations about life in the present and in the future.[2] Social status is usually described as coming from three sources:

1. Property—your economic position. How much money and "stuff" you have.
2. Prestige—how much respect and significance you have regardless of wealth. (This is where most youth ministers get social status despite their salaries.)
3. Power—the ability to "get your way" and control your resources and future.[3]

Social class is shaped (and reshaped) by where we live, who lives with us, our access to technology, and the quality of our education. English-speaking youth in Singapore have more opportunities than Mandarin-speaking youth there. Not only does their English fluency enhance their university opportunities, it also gives them access to broader, more powerful, and wealthier networks. And a student in Dublin, Ohio, will receive a dramatically different quality of educational support and opportunity than a student in downtown Cleveland, just 100 miles away.[4] Each school will have a different set of expectations and assumptions for their students, reinforcing class distinctions between the two schools. Students are often "tracked" into upper- and lower-level courses early in their elementary education process. Some of the markers for this are less about ability and more about how they talk to and respect adults, how they look, and who their parents are. A school district's test scores are less a reflection of a school's effectiveness and the students' IQs and more a reflection of the dominant social status in the community.

When I (Terry) was a kid, my friend Lee was extremely bright but overlooked. Lee came from a single-parent home outside of town. His mom couldn't spend a lot of time working with him on reading and homework, so his vocabulary and language development were behind the rest of us. Our fifth-grade teachers selected 10 students for an advanced class, and Lee was excluded. That was the beginning of the school telling Lee where he "ranked." Seven years later, I sat with Lee at our senior party. I was taken by his maturity, his ability to empathize with me, and his conversational skills. I think the school missed Lee's potential.

Unfortunately, Lee's situation mirrors what happens in many youth ministries, too. We "track" students into peer-leadership teams based on factors that often don't resemble how Jesus selected the 12 disciples. We subconsciously respond to social status and their parents' level of influence. We like achievement-oriented kids who are likely to volunteer for short-term mission trips. But is that what it means to "disciple"? We need to step back from our cultural patterns and see our communities as Christ wants us to see them.

A BRIEF HISTORY

Divisions along the lines of social status are not a new issue. There are countless examples throughout the Scriptures of how society valued the poor and rich differently (Leviticus 19:15; James 2:2-7). One of the things that most incited Christ's contemporaries was the way he turned all these distinctions upside down. He was born into a lower-class home with parents who couldn't even afford the legitimate lamb and pigeon sacrifice at his circumcision. Couldn't God have come into a family with a little more prestige than that? As Jesus moved into his own ministry, he spent time with the "unclean," tax collectors, adulterers—the list keeps going. He was always working on behalf of the underdog.

Classism lived on in the early church. Paul's critique to the Corinthians (1 Corinthians 11:17-34) was centered on confronting social divisions within the church. Influenced by Greco-Roman culture, many of the Corinthian Christians neglected the poor and vulnerable members of their congregation. Some were getting drunk while others went hungry. This definitely seems to be a "class" distinction.

Social divisions within the church also factored into the collections taken for the Jerusalem Church (Romans 15, 1 Corinthians 8-9, Galatians 6). Paul wanted the Gentile Christians and Judean Christians to have solidarity—accepting each other as equal but different. He challenged the financially rich Gentiles to embrace the culturally rich Jews (who shared the heritage of the Messiah) and vice versa.

We hope many of our readers include youth workers from outside the U.S., but it's worth saying just a word here to our fellow American youth workers about the implicit resistance in our own culture toward addressing the issues of social class. Core to the American dream is the idea that anyone can climb the ladder of success through a good education, hard work, and persistence. This makes for a great storyline, but it rarely happens without the corresponding benefit of social networks. But we're given the impression that all people can rise up and make something of themselves; so when we see someone struggling in poverty, the temptation is to look at the person and say, "Pull yourself up by your own bootstraps." This is nearly impossible for many Americans who've received an inferior education and who don't know people in power. Think about your students: To what degree are their successes reflections of their upbringings (e.g., soccer camp and art classes), where they went to school, and who they know?

Ministry across social barriers is difficult, and the returns are often small. If we want to be significant in ministry (with "prestige"), there isn't much promise of that unless we minister to and with people of higher social status. It's also tempting to get more excited about the big names in youth ministry and the cool sound system and café in the youth room than providing safe havens for kids from different social classes. Youth ministry needs to break from its long history of reinforcing social class distinctions and become a place where everyone is truly welcome, regardless of which side of the tracks you reside on.

SOCIAL CLASS AND YOU

Once we understand some of the ways social class plays out in youth ministry, then we need to think about our own social status. Granted, most people in youth ministry don't feel as though they're living the high life. But social class isn't something that occurs only among our youth—we all fall somewhere along the social ladder.

Even those of us struggling to pay our bills have a higher social status than we think. Did you go to college? Attending a four-year residential college is one of the great socializing forces toward upper-class levels. Most people in the world—including the U.S.—do not graduate from college. About 67 percent of American high school students attend a college and not quite half of those actually graduate.[5]

Can you control your future and resources? If you wanted to vacation in a sunny spot next year, could you? Can you go to the store and buy anyone in your family a new outfit? When's the last time you ate out? If you want to find a new job, who in your network can you call who might be connected to people who could hire you? The property, prestige, and power of most people in youth ministry far exceed those from the so-called "lower class" in your area.

Once we become more aware of our own social class, it affects how we see our local communities and the world. We can use our status to help others, whether it's helping someone find a job, sharing our second car while we're on vacation, or giving the Sophias of the world value by simply spending time with them.

To what degree is our contentment and joy in Christ connected to the comforts we enjoy from our social status? We readily quote, "For I can do everything with the help of Christ who gives me the strength I need" (Philippians 4:13, NLT). But what about Paul's words right before this? "I know how to live on almost nothing or with everything. I have learned the secret of living in every situation, whether it is with a full stomach or empty, with plenty or little" (Philippians 4:12-13). Most of us would prefer to be content "with everything" rather than with nothing, but Paul says he's learned contentment in all situations.

Examine your own contentment. One of the underlying problems is that many of us live in a society built upon consumerism—we have an ingrained discontent with what we have, so we work harder to get more stuff. Globalization continually raises the standard of what everyone should "have," and what used to be considered only an option for the upper class has now become standard fare for many middle-class people—overseas vacations, sprawling estates, high-tech gadgets, vacation homes, frequent eating out, etc. A new "can't live without" list has emerged. The size of our big-screen televisions is almost laughable, but they often serve as the focal points in our homes, symbols of our "bigger is better" consumerist culture.[6]

Hey, hang in there with us. We're not saying it's bad to get a new TV or spend spring break on the beach; but we need to acknowledge the continual rise in the standard of living most of us expect and notice the subtle ways that impacts the way we do youth ministry. We need to take Paul's words to heart: *Godliness with contentment is great gain. For we brought nothing into the world, and we can take nothing out of it. But if we have food and clothing, we will be content with that* (1 Timothy 6:6-8). To what degree is upward mobility an underlying issue for you? When is enough enough? Do you really need that new car, outfit, or bigger home? These are difficult issues to be sorted through in community, but we really need to confront our own consumerist practices as a first step toward dealing with the issues of social class in our own lives.

Class divides people, and it's a form or disunity rarely discussed in most churches. It's as if we're somehow afraid to talk about social status because it creates discomfort and cramps our style. It may mean inviting some people into our happy circle who make us feel uncomfortable. And when we *do* reach out beyond the borders to the community, we often don't know what to do with people when they show up on our ministry's doorstep.

The challenge to move beyond the borders of social class begins with each of us. One of the most transformative times during my time as a youth ministry rookie was when I (Terry) dropped off a student at his house and was startled to see how he lived. I never would've guessed he lived in a run-down home, but it opened my eyes to something I missed when I interacted with him at our youth events. The big turning point for my family was when we took in some teenagers to live with us. One girl who lived with us for a while was on welfare. She introduced us to her social circle, all people who lived in our community, but who'd been previously invisible to us. I never saw my community the same way after that. Next thing I knew, I was forming relationships with homeless people in our town. I became a better youth worker, parent, and disciple of Jesus as a result of crossing these social barriers. And hopefully God used us to bring the hope and love of Christ into some more lives beyond the borders of our typical comfort zone. We need to look for ways to reach across the chasm of social status to minister to students and families all up and down the social ladder.

WHAT CAN WE DO?

Dealing with the social status of our youth ministries and us as individuals requires a long-term commitment. And the answer for most of us isn't to get rid of everything we have and break ties with all of our networks and "power." But how can we use our power, prestige, and property to connect underprivileged youth with jobs, scholarships, tutoring, etc.? Here are a few ways we suggest responding to the barriers of pride and prejudice in youth ministry:

Expose the Invisible at Home

Help youth see that the struggles faced by individuals they encounter on a short-term mission trip might be similar to ones faced by invisible members of their community. Teach them about the ways neighborhoods are divided economically, ethnically, and thus, socially. Rewrite James 2:1-13 in your own words as if James were writing it to you and your youth ministry.

Teach about Global Issues

One of the ways to empower underprivileged kids is by giving them exposure to what's happening globally. Kids in many middle-class homes have dinner conversations with their parents about current events, and that gives them a leg up at school and in social networks. So share this privilege with kids who won't otherwise have it. Find ways to bring them on short-term mission trips. Most university, study-abroad students are almost exclusively from upper-middle-class homes because of the finances required. As a result of short-term missions, youth ministry has a better track record of exposing kids to the globe who would otherwise never get the experience of traveling abroad.

Emphasize Outreach

Youth groups who emphasize outreach have higher levels of social and ethnic diversity in their groups.[7] Cast a vision for reaching out to *all* the youth in your community—not just the ones who fit the predominant status and class of your church.

Listen to Stories

Spend time learning from people who are different from you. This is a necessary ongoing practice for our social-class awareness. Who do you avoid? Why do you avoid them? Our hunch is that in many cases, this is related to borders of social status. Therefore, get involved—and up close. Once you gain solidarity with people where they live, it can change your life.

Beware of "Tracking"

Do some students feel alienated because you didn't pick them for certain groups? You'll be surprised who may feel as though you don't care, and that they aren't "in" with your group. When you select students for particular activities, what criteria do you use? Do a quick analysis of which kids have gained your favor and preference. What if you broadened the pool of teens you select for various privileges?

FINAL THOUGHTS

Most of the popular youth ministry models were developed in predominantly white, upper-class neighborhoods outside of large cities. Publishers don't print many books that deal with ministry in urban, lower-class, or rural settings. Reaching beyond the borders of mainstream, middle-class youth requires a great deal of prayer, innovation, and concentrated effort.

Still, talking about social class makes most of us uncomfortable. After all, it's not as if most of us are living the sweet life. And what can we actually do about something that runs so deep?

We have great hope for what youth workers can do to address this issue. Youth ministry is notorious for getting into trouble with church leaders and parents when they start to widen the scope of their ministries. As we become more aware of social class—and help our youth do so as well—we tap into a powerful tool for helping kids deal with their own status, pay attention to the way it impacts others, and become agents of change to express the love of Jesus regardless of social status.

RESOURCES

And Still We Rise: The Trials and Triumphs of Twelve Gifted Inner-City Students by Miles Corwin (New York: Harper Perennial, 2001).

Limbo: Blue-Collar Roots, White-Collar Dreams by Alfred Lubrano (Hoboken, NJ: Wiley Press, 2003).

"Reconciliation Across Social Class" by Andrew Sears (http://www.urbanministry.org/reconciliation-across-social-class).

Search Institute (40 Developmental Assets that adolescents need to thrive): http://www.search-institute.org.

Movies (review which ones are suitable to share with your students)

Educating Rita
People Like Us: Social Class in America
The Pursuit of Happyness
Sense and Sensibility
Slumdog Millionaire

CHAPTER 10

SATAN'S SCHEMES

ETHNIC DIVISION
(WITH ERIC IVERSON)

Eric Iverson is a native of Minneapolis, Minnesota, where he lives with his wife, Judy, and their children, Hope and Isaiah Justice. A 25-year youth ministry veteran, Eric is a proud product of an urban church and serves as director of multicultural integrity for YouthWorks!, Inc. Eric consults, teaches, and trains nationally around issues of poverty, race, justice, and multiethnic ministry.

CASE STUDY

An African American man published the following letter in *Christianity Today* in 1971. As you read it, what issues emerge for you? Pay attention to how you respond to his perspective:

> Dear White Person:
>
> Although we have known each other for centuries, we have not truly known each other. I, the black person, feel I know more about you because I had to . . . It seems to me that our society is presently paying for the many years of wrongs done to the black person . . . In my rational moments, I can understand that you are a product of your forefather's

teachings, and are not entirely to blame for your feelings toward me. But if you or I should pass feelings of racial hatred to our children, we stand condemned before God . . .

You have made me doubt my ability to compete with you intellectually, and you keep stunting this area of my life with inferior school systems . . . Evaluate your life experiences and see how they may have given you your views of the black person . . . If that happens, it will enable us to love and to live together and enjoy the blessing God intended us to share.

Your fellow human being and future friend,

The Black Person[1]

Now spend a minute reading these Indicators of Privilege. See how many apply to you:

- If I wish, I can arrange to be in the company of people of my own race most of the time.
- I can turn on the television or look at the front page of the newspaper and see people of my race widely and positively represented.
- I can avoid spending time with people whom I was trained to mistrust and who have learned to mistrust my kind or me.
- If my family needs to move, we can be pretty sure of renting or purchasing housing in an affordable area where we want to live. We can be reasonably sure our new neighbors will be neutral or pleasant to us.
- I can be sure I will receive materials at school that reflect my heritage and race.
- Whether I pay for something, I can be confident my skin color won't work against the appearance that I'm financially reliable.
- I can forego deodorant today and not have people attribute my body odor to my race.
- If I graduate with honors, I can be confident I won't be called a "credit to my race."
- If a traffic cop pulls me over or if I am questioned by the mall security, I can be sure I haven't been singled out because of my race.
- I can be confident that when I walk into my church, I'll see people in leadership who look like me.

- I can choose bandages in "flesh" color and have them more or less match my skin.[2]

Questions for Further Reflection and Discussion

- What surprises you about the letter or going through the checklist?
- With what do you agree or disagree?
- What are the implications of this letter and these Indicators for your youth group?

I (Eric) am an African-American man. My grandfather was white, and whenever I used to travel with him from the city to rural communities, I got the "look" from the white people who lived there (i.e., everyone). I could see it in their eyes: *That kid must have been adopted*. It was clear I didn't really belong, even alongside my granddad. When I was a teenager, I was walking down the street one day with my mom (who's white), and the police officer asked her, "Hey, lady! Is this your pimp?" Then there was the time I showed up at camp with my youth group, and the message I heard clearly was, "If anything comes up missing this week, we know who did it." This is my life. I'm conscious of the color of my skin everywhere I go. I have to be. And now that I'm a dad, I think about it for my kids. I'm not looking for a fight or expecting some special favor. I'm not angry and getting ready to burn down someone's house. But the color of my skin impacts everything I do—and so does yours. If you're from the dominant Euro-American culture (white), you probably don't think about your skin color as much as I do. But if your youth ministry is going to truly move beyond borders, it must seriously engage with this issue of race.

The Great Commission (make disciples of all nations) and the Great Commandment (love God and others) make up the core of the gospel. We may argue about many things, but it's safe to say these two directives are central to how we as Christians live out our faith and ministry. Our churches and youth ministries ought to be pictures of the Great Commission and the Great Commandment—places filled with people from a diversity of cultures who are being discipled and making disciples. Yet, as already pointed out, most North American ministries are extremely segregated—and this is one of the major roadblocks to living out the gospel today. The connections between race and social class are abundant. But there are some specific dimensions to each form of prejudice, so that's why we've dealt with them over two chapters.

We'll begin with the evil origins of race. Then we'll look at some ways racism runs deeply through youth ministry and suggest some ways to deal with it.

RACE

I not only want to tear down racism, but also eliminate the whole made-up concept of race. *Race* is an artificial classification that is intolerable today, especially as people migrate across more and more cultural boundaries. The U.S. Census Bureau has five "race alone" categories: Black/African-American, White, American Indian and Alaska Native, Asian, Native Hawaiian and Pacific Islander, and Other[3]; then there are 63 other "race alone or in combination" categories—collections of smaller ethnic or national origin subgroups.[4] Confused yet? I am every time I fill out one of these forms.

Ethnic division has a long, seedy history. The Old Testament is rife with one tribe or nation pummeling another just because its people looked different. And this evil has continued throughout all civilizations. For example, when the English invaded Ireland, they called the Irish "white monkeys," which seemed to help the English feel more entitled to conquering the Emerald Isle for themselves. But the idea of developing a whole classification for people according to their ethnicity (a.k.a. labeling people by "race") is a relatively recent phenomenon with origins in the early years of the United States. Racial categories were created largely to help Christians rationalize slave ownership, all in the name of "progress." Your racial category determined your status and made it clear who were slaves and who were the benefactors of slave labor.

Presidents Thomas Jefferson and Andrew Jackson knew there was something troubling about this idea, so they insisted upon some research to back it up. Jefferson told scientists to find data supporting the idea that blacks "are inferior to the whites in the endowments both of body and mind. It is not against experience to suppose, that different species . . . may possess different qualifications."[5] He wanted to root racial distinction biologically. The assumption was that hierarchy according to race was part of God's design and impossible to change. And since Africans were genetically not as smart or morally apt as Europeans, "stewarding" them as slaves didn't seem so bad.

Taking this a step further, Andrew Jackson said Native Americans had "neither the intelligence, the industry, the moral habits, nor the desire of improvement which are essential to any favorable change . . . Established in the midst of another and a superior race, they must necessarily yield to the force of circumstances and ere long disappear."[6] These men's views became justification for owning or exterminating certain human beings, all in the name of "progress."

The study and promotion of race distinction continued after Samuel George Morton developed an intelligence ranking based upon the "science" of craniometry—a process of filling empty skulls with mustard seeds. The hypothesis was: The more seeds in the skulls, the smarter the race. Morton discovered that since the skulls of European-American men contained the most mustard seeds, they were the most intelligent people on earth. As far-fetched as these ideas sound, they became etched into the systems and ideas about what was "normal and appropriate treatment" for various groups of people.

Racial classifications are artificial and not the way God intended us to be identified. These classifications can and must be dismantled and replaced with seeing people first as image-bearers of God. The change begins with you and your youth.

RACE AND YOUTH MINISTRY

My fear is that the church has unknowingly bought into these lies about the "natural order of things" where some people just aren't as smart or can't be as "successful" as others. Many ministry leaders feel as though discussions about race just end up alienating people, and they want us to move beyond the global conversation. But we can't just sweep under the carpet the realities in the U.S.:

	White	African-American
Percentage of families below poverty line	7.2	21.8
Median income	$60,000	$35,000
High school graduation rate	78 percent	55 percent

Source: Black-White Gap in the U.S. (U.S. Census, Manhattan Institute for Policy Research)

It's hard to deny the numbers. Do black kids really lack so much intelligence that half never graduate from high school? And are white kids so much smarter? Do the income differences really point to different work ethics, or is there something deeper that explains this?

One of the most important books exposing racism among U.S. Christians is *Divided by Faith* by Michael Emerson and Christian Smith. The book is based upon extensive research of how white evangelicals in the U.S. are addressing the issues of race and ethnicity.

Debbie, one of the women interviewed in the book, expresses the commonly held white, evangelical perspective about race when she responds to the question, "Does our country have a race problem?" She replied, "I think we make it a problem."[7] When asked to expand, she explained:

> Well to me, people have problems. I mean, two white guys working together are gonna have arguments once in awhile. Women are gonna have arguments. It happens between men and women, between two white guys and two white women. It's just people. People are going to have arguments with people. I feel like once in a while, when an argument happens, say between a black guy and a white guy, instead of saying, "Hey, there are two guys having an argument," we say it's a race issue.[8]

Another white woman responding to the same question said,

> We have tried for thirty years to become a unified nation and now it is a big black push to be separate again. You know, like the Million Man March was for separation. It is very frustrating. I am not racist and I don't notice my friend's color. But it is frustrating when "Oh, this is black heritage month, and this is Asian awareness and this is . . ." Well when is there a basic white month?"[9]

Both of these women, like most of the white evangelicals in Emerson and Smith's large sample, compartmentalized race as a marginal issue because it was not a central part of their day-to-day lives. Emerson and Smith conclude, "White evangelicalism likely does more to perpetuate the racialized society than to reduce it."[10] And white conservative Protestants "are more than twice as likely as other whites to blame lack of equality (e.g. differences in income) between blacks and whites on a *lack of motivation and work ethic than upon discrimination*" (emphasis added).[11]

There are similar strands to how racism plays out in other parts of the world. The rifts between Afrikaans, so-called colored, black, and Indian youth continue to challenge many South African churches and youth ministries. Palestinian Christians often feel ostracized by pro-Israeli Christians in the West. Many Singaporean youth from Indian descent feel like lower-class citizens compared to the Singaporean youth from Chinese descent in their schools and youth groups. Satan is having a heyday with ethnic division.

For churches that decide to address the issue of racism head-on, the greatest resistance comes from parents of teenagers. The problem isn't usually found in discussing the issue theologically; it shows up when churches decide to become more inclusive. Parents of teenagers aren't sure they want their kids spending time with "those" kids, much less dating them. But with the transforming power of Christ, many ministries are beginning to overcome the barriers of history, prejudice, and fear to better reflect the beautiful diversity of Christ's body.

LEVERAGING SHORT-TERM MISSIONS TO CONFRONT RACISM

Short-term missions can powerfully shape (for good or bad) the way we view people from different cultural backgrounds. I (Eric) spend a lot of time thinking about this issue in my work as the director of multicultural integrity for a large short-term mission agency that organizes cross-cultural experiences for thousands of youth groups every summer.

One summer we worked with a Euro-American youth group from Hyde Park, an affluent Chicago neighborhood (picture the Obama's house before they moved to the White House). We sent this group to Birmingham, Alabama. One of the youth leader's primary goals was to expose his Chicago-area students to racism and poverty. He was disappointed with our efforts, and a pretty critical letter showed up on my desk. The leader's critique was as follows:

- The design of programming at the mission site should have been more deliberate in fostering our students' understanding of race and racial issues.
- More effort was needed to help our students confront their negative and inaccurate stereotypes of the African-Americans they encountered.
- The focus of the work was exclusively *to* the local people rather than serving the local community together and learning from the locals.
- None of your staff members who worked with us is a person of color.

My follow-up phone conversation with this youth leader was a big aha moment for me. He summarized his critique again and then went on to tell me that in spite of the challenges, the trip was a turning point for his group members. Through his own initiative, he worked hard to help his students develop true friendships with some of the locals—all of whom were African-Americans. He talked with his students about the ongoing realities of slavery more than a century after the Civil War. And he helped them see how these challenges exist for people living a few blocks from their church in Chicago.

My conversation with this leader happened just after Hurricane Katrina had ravaged the Gulf Coast. Like the rest of the country, this suburban youth group watched the drama unfold as people suffered for days until help arrived. It was obvious that almost all the people who were stranded were people of color. The students were horrified as they saw the fate of people who looked so much like their new friends in Birmingham. They watched with horror as they saw mostly African-Americans stranded on rooftops, begging to leave, and worst of all, floating facedown in the water. The people they watched on the news from New Orleans were no longer "those people" suffering but "*our* people." The youth leader was surprised by the deep sense of indignation among his students as they reacted to the injustice. Something had definitely changed.

The upper middle-class students from Hyde Park were changed by humbly serving with people in Alabama who looked different than them. The unconscious hierarchal classification the students held for poor African-Americans from the South was shaken. When we identify suffering people as our friends, their problem becomes *our* problem. Apathy is less common when we share the problem.

When we encounter someone for the first time, our brains instantly decide if the person is friend or foe, safe or dangerous, in our tribe or out of it, and valuable or worthless. These students created a new classification for people who looked like their new friends from Birmingham. They were forced to rethink their subconscious categories—or at least become more aware of those categories and the impact they have upon how they live out their faith. I'm convinced this largely came as a result of the discipling this group received from their youth leader. In other words: Just taking students to ethnically different communities doesn't automatically bring about this kind of transformation; but the aforementioned intentional conversation can help your students process these experiences and transfer them back home.

The experience with this church put me on a journey of figuring out how we can more intentionally use short-term experiences to help North American youth ministries alter their views of people from different ethnic backgrounds, no matter where they live—Mexico, Birmingham, or around the corner. Short-term mission trips offer us tremendous opportunities to reach with Christ's love across the evil divide of race. Just as our youth ministries need to lead the way in embracing people from different social statuses, so we must do so across ethnic differences as well. The goal is not to ignore our differences but learn from them, better understand who Christ is as a result of them, and together reflect the kingdom of God.

WHAT CAN WE DO?

Just as with social class, dealing with the issues of race and its negative impact requires a lot of perseverance. If it's too much, get help or please just move on for now, because any effort to deal with it will only frustrate you, and you'll probably quit before you get very far. If you believe you're ready to move forward, hold your hands straight out in front of you, palms up. The Holy Spirit is going to be in charge. Let the Spirit drive this.

Give It Time

Accept the fact this will take a lot of time and perseverance. It will be risky for you, and you may lose friends and students over it. So start slowly—gradually weave this into your conversations. Inject your teaching with this. Most of us have the power to ignore race, but we typically focus on it instead. Start asking questions for yourself and then ask your youth to do the same.

Journal Your Observations for a Week

As you encounter different people throughout your day, ask yourself the following questions:

- How do I assign meaning to the physical characteristics of the people I see? What does their appearance say to me about who they are?
- What does skin color tell me about motives, safety, intelligence, personality, occupation, ambition, or morality?

- What is going on in me below the surface? What are my thought patterns about what I see, hear, or read? How am I drawing these conclusions (right or wrong)? How much time do they take to formulate?
- Where do these perceptions come from? How are they formed and enforced in my mind?

Integrate into Programming and Teaching

Your goal is to facilitate discovery, not deposit knowledge. By raising awareness about the impact of race, we begin to eliminate its power to divide us. Seeing how it has influenced communities where you serve or where we live allows our youth to keep their focus on loving God and loving others. Have students research and report on the community's past and present as it relates to this issue (for U.S. communities, check out http://factfinder.census.gov/home/saff/main.html). And beware of the subtle ways you can teach about this. Point out that the Ethiopian eunuch was probably a black man (Acts 8:26-40). Be sure your examples and case studies aren't just about white, middle-class issues and names. And get rid of any and all pictures of Jesus as a "white" guy from Europe! His Middle Eastern ethnicity ought to be appropriately represented in the images we portray.

Evaluate Your Worship Style

The way you sing, pray, and lead worship comes from an ethnic tradition. Musical styles, the way your group prays, and the ways your leaders interact with your group are all developed within a culture. Music is not culturally neutral. If you're serious about developing a diverse ministry, then get a diverse group of adults and students together and just ask the question, "How can our worship style be more inclusive? We're going to spend all of eternity worshiping with people from every nation and tribe, speaking every language (Revelation 7:9-10). So let's start the rehearsal!" You can have fun leading your group into new and dynamic ways to worship God in your ministry.

Diversify Leadership

Minority students are scanning your leadership teams (youth and adults) to see if there's a place for them. You'll develop a different kind of ministry when you have ethnic (and social!) diversity among your leadership.

Create opportunities for minority leaders to teach—and not just about racism. Hearing an African-American or Latino leader teach a Bible study about sex, finances, and peer pressure is often far more powerful than having them just teach about racism or classism all the time.

Don't Tolerate Any Forms of Ethnic Jokes

Develop a zero-tolerance policy for inappropriate jokes and language directed toward any ethnic group. Don't allow anyone to serve in a leadership position who doesn't share your commitment to this value.

FINAL THOUGHTS

It's troubling that conversations about multiculturalism and racism are more often heard in sociology classrooms at Big Ten universities and among political pundits on TV than among Christian leaders. Yet there's nowhere that honest conversations about the issues of racism and prejudice should feel more natural than in churches. Many youth ministries are leading the way. They know this isn't just a politically correct topic, but one that highlights whether or not we're committed to true discipleship.

Many youth today are far more accepting of people from different ethnic backgrounds than their parents were. But the work isn't over. There are often subtle issues of racism and discrimination that lurk beneath the surface. Go there with your teenagers. Learn about this together. And discover the beautiful diversity that exists beyond the borders of your own skin.

RESOURCES

Being White: Stories of Race and Racism by Karyn D. McKinley (Routledge, 2005).

Cultural Intelligence: Improving Your CQ to Engage Our Multicultural World by David Livermore (Baker, 2009).

Deep Justice Journeys: Moving from Missions Trips to Missional Living by Kara Powell and Brad M. Griffin (Zondervan/YS, 2009).

Divided by Faith: Evangelical Religion and the Problem of Race in America by Michael O. Emerson and Christian Smith (New York: Oxford University Press, 2000).

The Elusive Dream: The Power of Race in Interracial Churches by Korie L. Edwards (Oxford, 2008).

One Body, One Spirit: Principles of Successful Multiracial Churches by George Yancey (InterVarsity Press, 2203).

United by Faith by Curtiss Paul DeYoung, Michael O. Emerson, George Yancey, and Karen Chai Kim (Oxford, 2003).

"So You Think You're an Anti-Racist?" by Paul C. Gorski (http://www.edchange.org/handouts/paradigmshifts_race.pdf).

U.S. Census Data (http://factfinder.census.gov/home/saff/main.html).

CHAPTER 11

HOLLYWOOD VERSUS JIHAD

CLASH OF CIVILIZATIONS

CASE STUDY

Ahmed Shah, a shy and introverted 17 year old, preferred the solace of his room to the chatter of his friends. His father, Yusuf Shah, was a schoolteacher. He said Ahmed usually spent his time studying so he could become a doctor. Ahmed even got himself photographed wearing a doctor's coat and a stethoscope and kept the framed picture in his room.

Ahmed was the youngest of three brothers in this traditional Pakistani family. There were always people coming and going from their home, so Ahmed's increased presence at the mosque next door pretty much went unnoticed. His parents were happy to see his heightened interest in religion, but they grew somewhat concerned when they saw his devotion grow to the point of fanaticism. Every night he read the Qur'an by candlelight, often reading aloud and crying.

One day Ahmed suddenly left home without warning. Three weeks later, he called his father and said, "*Abbu, mein jaa raha hoon*" ("Dad, I'm leaving"). A few hours later, the Shahs heard security vehicles screech to a halt outside their door. Their son, they were told, had exploded himself at the army headquarters in Kashmir. Neighbors were shocked that the shy, quiet boy who they assumed wanted nothing more than to be a doctor turned out to be a suicide bomber. After driving a stolen car laden with explosives into the high-security barrier, all that remained of Ahmed's body were fragmented pieces blown over a distance of 100 meters.[1]

Questions for Further Reflection and Discussion

- What emotions surface as you read this and other stories like it? How do you feel toward Ahmed? His father?
- What do you think suicide bombers like Ahmed are trying to accomplish?
- In what ways do the stories of suicide bombers affect your life?

Back when we served full time as youth pastors, few if any of our students were familiar with terms such as *al-Qaeda, jihad*, and *suicide bomber*. For that matter, even *war* was primarily understood as a topic in social studies class—not a concept that directly affected our lives. But 9/11 changed everything. All of us were deeply marked by it. *Terrorism* became a household word for our students and their families, even if it at times feels somewhat removed.

The issue at stake in this chapter—the clash of pluralistic Western culture with fundamentalist religious cultures—might feel less tangible than many of the other issues addressed in the book. At some level we can quickly sympathize with the downside of poverty, racism, and disease; but it's really difficult to get our minds around just what's behind the war on terror and the origins of the conflicts. Today's battles are not primarily between governments but between cultural ideologies. In particular, the Western world is convinced that the freedoms of pluralism, equality, economic development, and technology should be the rights of *all* people. In contrast, religious fundamentalists are equally convinced that globalization is the new brand of cultural imperialism invading their shores. Both sides believe they're correct. This conflict creates real-life challenges for people all over the world. And everything suggests this is going to continue to be a growing issue for our students as they embark on life as adult citizens, parents, and professionals.

The predominant powers in the world are multinational corporations and fundamentalist movements, not federal governments or groups like the United Nations. Devout Islamic youth have little loyalty to their countries; their allegiance is solely to Allah—nationality and citizenship mean very little. Their religion is at the core of their identities. In a similar way, to a "devout" Western young person, being a "Canadian" or "Brit" means little compared to identifying with the clothes you wear and the music you like. Their allegiance is to brands, sports teams, superstars, and hobbies.

Many of the largest multinational corporations are trying to sell a pluralistic "have it your way" reality. The aim is largely to remove borders and local identities and create a universal appetite for the same foods, entertainment, and products. On the other hand, many tribes operate by a fundamentalist perspective that says, "Our way is the only way, and we'll rule based upon that premise." These tribes redraw boundaries in order to divide, whether it's Kurdish Iraq, Islamic Sudan, or the Tutsi/Hutu rift that eliminated so many lives in Rwanda.

Christians committed to the universals of the Bible find themselves in an interesting quandary. Surely we don't affirm the seemingly malicious and oppressive pursuits of the Taliban, but neither do we celebrate a pleasure-driven consumerism invading local communities near and far. We want to use this chapter to highlight a few of the key threads that run through this growing clash of civilizations. We'll provide an overview of both sides of the clash—globalization versus tribalism, the inevitable terrorism that ensues, the implications for Western Christians, and some practical ways to address this complex issue in student ministry.

"ALL ROADS LEAD TO HEAVEN" VERSUS "MY WAY OR THE HIGHWAY"

Western civilization was founded upon scientific freedom and the benefits of many different forms of art, literature, and music. Initially the leaders of Christianity, Islam, and Judaism were equally concerned about the inevitable relativism that could emerge from this modern movement. But by the 16th century, Christian priests and Jewish rabbis reconciled this dilemma by leading the way in creating a clear separation between government and religion. With time, Christian and Jewish leaders and scholars wholeheartedly embraced the diversity of thinking fueled by this Cultural Revolution. Islamic clerics, however, never shared the view of their Christian and Jewish peers; they were determined to remain pure from the pluralistic ills of modernity and Western civilization.

Meanwhile, the continued progression of Western culture combined with the increased opportunity for people to move from one place to another led to a growing spirit of pluralism—the idea that there's no single "right" way to view the world. The driving agenda was to encourage multiple and conflicting opinions and philosophies. As a result, the influence of majority religious groups diminished, and values such as tolerance, dialogue, compassion, and multiple ways of seeing the world flourished.

Pluralistic thinking has been around for hundreds of years among philosophers and in universities; but only in the last few decades has this thinking really started to take hold at grassroots levels. And with the advent of postmodernism, the emphasis is upon areas of agreement rather than points of difference. The sharp edges and distinctions are downplayed and commonalities emphasized. As an example, a prominent study found that 44 percent of Americans believe "The Bible, the Koran and the Book of Mormon are different expressions of the same spiritual truths."[2]

On the other side of the civilization clash are those who come from an exclusivist perspective—they believe in universal truths and morals, not the will or preferences of culture. The sacred text has the final say. Ironically, many fundamentalist Muslims are confused by Christians who they perceive to be pluralistic.

Christianity, Judaism, and Islam are the three predominant, monotheistic religions in the world. As just noted, Islamic *imams* never embraced pluralistic thinking the way Christian and Jewish leaders did. Instead they retained a religious zeal to see states governed by Sharia law.[3] Most Islamic leaders resist much emphasis on contextualization and reimagining their faith; in fact, many of these leaders have incredible disdain for the West because the decadent pleasures of Western globalization are luring the faithful away from Islam. It's here, at the nexus of pluralistic globalization and fundamentalist tribalism, that we find the epicenter of today's greatest conflicts.

FUNDAMENTALISM + GLOBALIZATION = TERRORISM

Both globalization and fundamentalist-based religion have a mutual relationship with terrorism. Traditionally, *religious violence* meant attacking other faith's houses of worship, including temple burnings, mosque bombings, and church lynchings. Today fundamentalist religious groups are ironically using the technological advances of globalization to provide them with new weapons and an international audience. For example, Hollywood war films are used in terrorist teaching camps in Afghanistan.

The target of extremist groups is rarely the innocent victims only; it's also the Western viewers gripped by fear. They aim to destabilize economies and the clout of monolithic corporations and their corresponding governments. Globalization and the pluralistic blurring of ideologies and cultures are at the core of what extremist groups are reacting against. Sam George, an Indian-American Christian leader who has written broadly on this topic, says, "The products of globalization have found a perfect match for the intentions of terrorist groups, and the tug of war for the New World Order continues."[4]

Who are the terrorists? They're boys like Ahmed who, by tapping into a corrupt expression of Islam, see protecting the land as their moral duty. Terrorists include unemployed and angry Sikh youth who are experiencing a farm crisis that fuels a violent nationalism. They're Tamil Tigers equipped with cyanide capsules in Sri Lanka and extremists like Timothy McVeigh in Oklahoma City. Terrorist movements usually arise in response to injustices, real or imagined, that their members believe must be corrected.

Young men are at the forefront of terrorist movements. They're daring, looking for a cause, and determined. They're deeply spiritual and fervent in their quest for ultimate truth. Sam George describes them this way: "[Terrorists] include both poor school dropouts and university students, both idealists and devout seekers with a sense of something missing in their lives. They tend to be members of the financially and socially marginalized sections of society."[5]

Young people make ideal recruits because they're easy to indoctrinate. George goes on to say, "Within the first six months of the outbreak of war in Afghanistan in September 2001, it is believed that more youngsters *joined* the cause of Jihad that at any other time in history"[6] (bold word part of original text). Of course, the influential, passionate zeal of youth is attractive to recruiters, too—something we've seen continually throughout this book. But there's an underbelly to youth's revolutionary potential.

Terrorism is a characteristic of youth beyond Pakistan and Iran.

There's a growing culture of violent aggression on the rise among youth worldwide. Youth gangs, school shootings, media violence, and underground movements everywhere consist of similar populations of marginalized, disadvantaged youth. "Countless numbers of young people lay down their lives every year and become 'martyrs' for various ideological causes."[7]

As noted earlier, this isn't the nature of *most* youth today, but there are still far too many who are susceptible to finding their significance in all the wrong places. The continued growth of globalization through terrorism presents us with a timely challenge and responsibility. Before talking about some ways to respond, we need to address the blur of both extremes that occurs for Western Christians.

WESTERN CHRISTIANITY: A BLUR OF BOTH WORLDS

The terrorist examples most familiar to us come from Islamic extremist groups like al-Qaeda and Hamas. But again, this isn't simply a "Muslim thing." The underpinnings of fundamentalism and terrorism are as familiar to Christians, Hindus, and Jews as they are to Muslims. Of course, we readily point to the Crusades as an embarrassing "Christian" example of using terror to wield power in the clash of civilizations; but we don't have to look that far back, either, to get a picture of what this looks like. There are fundamentalist Christians today who burn mosques in India and bomb abortion clinics in the U.S.

Few of us would affirm this kind of violent response to pluralism, just as most Muslims are equally appalled by killings done in the name of Allah. But many of us also find dissonance when we connect our beliefs in Jesus and his universal claims with the growing pluralism of the globalized world. We, too, can see the problems with Western culture's indulgence in immorality, pornography, sexual perversion, and divorce. We worry about the impact of invading the world with a uniform array of products and programs from the Western world. But we differ with the terrorists in how to respond.

Other books more fully handle the topic of how we ought to live out our Christian faith in a pluralistic society.[8] Our interest here is to simply highlight the importance of this issue as a seminal concern for life in an increasingly borderless world. The clash between fundamentalism and pluralism will continue. A key part of discipling our students is helping them engage with this timely issue in tangible ways.

WHAT CAN WE DO?

Many are convinced that growing clashes between East and West, Muslim and Christian, and tribe and McWorld are inevitable. Only Jesus can redeem us from these evils, but his way of doing so includes people like you and your students. Here are a few suggestions for how to respond to this challenge:

Stimulate Conversation with Your Students

Most of your students are forming impressions about these issues, even if you rarely hear them talk about them or mention them on Facebook. Many of your students talk about this at school, they make judgments about what they see on the news, and they draw upon the storylines of *24* and *The Bourne Identity* to inform how they view Islam and Middle Easterners.

Youth can be motivated for terrorism, or they can be inspired to lay down their lives for Jesus. Loving our neighbor is not just something we say; it's how we view the world and live our lives. An endless clash between civilizations is hell on earth, and it's something we ought to inspire our youth to resist in whatever ways possible.[9] First educate yourself on the topics, then include them in Bible study discussions, conversations over coffee, and while doing service projects together.

Give Peace a Chance

Help students see how people like Mother Teresa and Martin Luther King passionately protested the ills of our modern world by living alternative lifestyles rooted in love, service, justice, and peace. Teach them to see the relevance of legislation and elections to how we promote peace. And most of all, elevate and model a lifestyle of peace and Christlike love.

Beware of Nationalism

Nationalism, the orientation that "our country is the best and most important," can be dangerous. First-century Jewish Christians, including Peter, had reason to believe their nation was the best. After all, God called the Israelites his "chosen people." Yet, even Peter had to be confronted (Acts 10) on his prejudice and realize that the gospel was for Gentiles, too. In the last century, nationalism in Germany fueled atrocities against other nations, and most Christians did little to stand in opposition.

When many of us were teenagers, "active military duty" was something our parents or grandparents did many years earlier, not something we committed to. The military interests of our nation were far removed from most of us. Today, many of our students have siblings, friends, cousins, and parents who are currently deployed, and the realities of war affect communities all over the nation. This has brought about an appropriate surge in the amount of appreciation we have for our military and their sacrificial service.

However, in our noble attempts to honor our military personnel, we can unintentionally communicate a nationalism that says the life of a fellow citizen is more important than a life on the other side of the world. Therefore, when praying for our soldiers, don't forget to pray for affected individuals and families in other nations. When talking about the devastating effects of war, report on the casualties among the Afghans as well as our soldiers.

Exhibiting some pride in our country and offering support to military personnel and government officials is appropriate when it aligns with Christian values. But when we repeat mantras that "we're the best nation in the world" (or worse yet, "God is on our side"), an unhealthy perspective can develop. We pray for God's blessing on America. We also pray for God's blessing upon the entire world.

Teach Interfaith Dialogue

World religions are more than an academic topic to address with students. To learn about Islam might mean understanding the faith of students sitting next to them in math class. Buddhism may be the worldview of the woman serving them Chinese food, or Hinduism the religion and culture of the neighbors across the street. Even if there are no mosques or temples in your community, these religions shape the faiths of many people in our neighborhoods.

Students must be prepared to engage in respectful dialogue with others. How can they find common ground where values are shared while still retaining their convictions? How can they be humble learners while also calling others to follow Jesus? We have to help students build strong identities and confidence regarding what it means to follow Jesus while simultaneously equipping them to engage in meaningful interaction with people of other faiths.

International Guest Speakers

One of the most practical steps is having Christians from other countries speak to your youth about global issues. Have them share about their cultures, believers in their home countries, and how they view the world. Seeing the planet through their eyes instead of simply through news headlines will broaden perspectives.

FINAL THOUGHTS

As our world becomes seamlessly connected through pop culture, it's simultaneously becoming more divided religiously and ethnically. Clearly we abhor the evils perpetuated by terrorism, but there's something to be learned by looking at the devotion and concerns behind their militant actions.

High schools are engaging students in conversations about these issues and, without question, university professors are sharing their convictions with incoming freshmen. Churches and youth ministries need to be doing this, too. A student ministry that cares about the world will consider the growing chasm between local tribal groups and multinational pluralistic groups. The Christian story, more than any other, provides a way to make meaning of all this. As we engage together in understanding the story of God and its application across every tribe, nation, and culture, we have a lens by which to move through the conflicting malaise of a terror-ridden world.

RESOURCES

Jihad vs. McWorld: Terrorism's Challenge to Democracy by Benjamin R. Barber (Ballantine Books, 1996).

Half the Sky: Turning Oppression into Opportunity for Women Worldwide by Nicholas D. Kristof and Sheryl Wu Dunn (Knopf, 2009).

Three Cups of Tea: One Man's Mission to Promote Peace . . . One School at a Time by Greg Mortenson and David Oliver Relin (Penguin Books, 2006).

One World or Many: The Impact of Globalisation on Mission edited by Richard Tiplady (William Carey Publishers, 2003).

Fundamentalism and Terrorism by Robert M. Young (http://www.human-nature.com/rmyoung/papers/pap135h.htm).

The Kite Runner by Khaled Hosseini (Riverhead Books, 2003) and the movie (Dreamworks, 2007).

PART 3
SERVE

We've covered a myriad of issues. We've worked hard to include practical action steps for each topic, but a large purpose behind this book has been about increasing your awareness of the realities happening in our world. And we've continued to say that "creating awareness" is a key way to respond to these issues. Effective and loving engagement with our neighbors near and far begins with a heightened understanding of their lives. In short, we can't do anything about things we don't know about.

But awareness by itself does little to change the lives of global youth who feel locked out of the in-group, kids trafficked for sex and labor, and families mired in disease and poverty. Eventually we have to do something more than be aware.

The final two chapters move us toward action. We begin by discussing how to make a difference both locally and globally. Then we conclude with a few thoughts about what can truly be done through teenagers in response to these issues.

CHAPTER 12

"GLOCAL SERVICE"

MAKING A DIFFERENCE NEAR AND FAR

Do you feel overwhelmed? Thinking, pondering, and wrestling with these issues can be exhausting and sometimes frustrating. Are we supposed to tackle all of them—and if not, how do we choose? Should we focus locally or globally? We promise not to give you five-cent answers to these million-dollar questions, but we'll try to point you in a few directions. We begin by looking at the value of a glocal perspective, an idea that we need to keep both local and global needs in view. Then we review some concrete steps for applying what we've covered throughout the book.

Economic disparity, racism, and classism exist near and far. Technology alters the lives of people from East to West. The clash between fundamentalism and globalization is felt in classrooms from Cleveland to Baghdad. Our views toward immigrants affect vendors at the local farmers' market and food stalls in Mexico City. TB and HIV/AIDS are killing South Africans, Russians, and Canadians. And teenagers are trafficked around the corner and 12 time zones away. All the issues we've covered in this book have local and global—or "glocal"—dimensions to them. We want to briefly summarize the concept of a glocal view and then suggest several ways to launch glocal responses to the issues addressed throughout the book.

A "GLOCAL" VIEW

Even if the term *glocal* is new to you, you're already pretty experienced with the idea.[1] Glocal is a way of capturing what we've been doing throughout this book when we've pointed out the local and global dimensions of each issue. Poverty isn't something that just happens "here," but neither is human trafficking something that happens "there" only. Our students are growing up in a glocal world:

Though they travel across international borders, they're indoctrinated with the mantra "buy local."

They're globally conscious, but also they want to support local coffee shops and independent bookstores. When they go overseas, they want to know if they can stay connected technologically to their local networks back home.

When they get home, they want to share photos with new friends overseas.

Our local coffee shops sell coffee from faraway places, and the local vintage boutiques sell clothes made in places like Bangladesh, Haiti, or Mexico.

The clear distinctions between local and global are gone. Multinational corporations are becoming more intentionally glocal. Coca-Cola recently started putting a local face—Bollywood actor Hrithik Roshan—on its advertisements in India. In fact, the series of Coke ads include so many Indian actors, props, music, and food that you almost forget Coca-Cola started as an American company. Yet there's an underlying message in the Indian ads that says Coke will connect you to a young, hip, Western vibe. This is what glocal looks like.

Missions experts and theologians have also realized the need to make the transcultural, global gospel something that connects up close, locally, and personally. Although the gospel is transcultural, it's always understood through a local time and place. "Mission has to be global in its vision, its strategy, and its content . . . [But] in order to be global, mission has to be contextual!"[2] With every issue in part 2, we stress the importance of encountering these issues—and the people they affect—up close: Build relationships with underprivileged people, learn the stories of nearby immigrants, and don't substitute texting for live conversations over coffee or rice and beans.

Our youth ministries are glocal entities. They're rooted in specific places and consist of kids and families from particular regions and communities—but also we're connected with Christians, products, and news events going on around the world. Some have compared this phenomenon to a desktop computer—it sits in one spot but is connected through the Internet to the globe.[3]

A GLOCAL RESPONSE

One of the things we love about the growth of short-term mission trips is that they've created fascinating transcontinental relationships between youth groups and churches around the world. More than ever before, we have unprecedented opportunities to serve with our brothers and sisters in Christ glocally to make a difference near and far. With a little effort, this opportunity can be used to reach beyond local and global borders. Here's what glocal service could look like for you and your youth:

Global: Support a ministry that prevents AIDS in Rwanda. Visit and serve as needed.

Local: Organize or participate in an AIDS walk in your community.

Global: Advocate for Sudan by organizing a letter-writing campaign to those in power, including congress people and the media.

Local: Recruit families in your church to host Sudanese refugees.

Global: Partner with a ministry in Thailand to offer English camps.

Local: Teach English to newly arrived immigrants in your town.

Global: Volunteer for a ministry that provides clean water to communities without it.

Local: Start a recycling program at your church and take a day to clean a local river.

There's no shortage of ways to get involved. But where do we begin? How do we figure out which of the many issues to take on? Here are a handful of next steps:

View Wide, Engage Deep

Much of our interest throughout this book has been to help broaden the global perspective of you and your students. We're convinced a widened perspective is a nonnegotiable for responsibly living out the gospel in the 21st-century world. That doesn't mean we should continually put ourselves on mind-numbing guilt trips for never doing enough. There are too many issues in too many places requiring too much attention for us to equally respond to all of them. We can't do everything.

Still, we can't think of an issue in this book that we shouldn't all *care* about. And at some level, we can all *do* something in response to most of them. For example, taking good care of the earth is something that starts with each of us; and it's reflected in how we drive, and what we do with our garbage. Standing up against racism and classism is something every follower of Jesus is called to do when we witness the oppressed getting slammed. We should all pray, vote, and live with these issues in mind. Then we need to prayerfully consider one or two issues and places where we can engage more deeply.

Pick an Issue

What issue specifically weighs on your heart? What cause seems unusually important to your group of students? How might some of the interests and experiences of your students be God's way of directing you toward the issue where you can most deeply engage? Learn all you can about the issue. Note the recommended resources in the chapter that deals with this issue (see part 2) and begin there. Enlist your students to be part of the learning process. Pray about the best way to engage in this cause.

Part of selecting an issue includes taking note of the interests, connections, and skill sets represented in your own group. Bob Roberts, pastor of Northwood Church in Dallas, is a leading proponent of a glocal mission strategy. One of his approaches is to encourage his people to use their vocational gifts to serve locally and overseas.[4] Northwood has sent schoolteachers to other nations to help locals start their own schools. Lawyers from his church have traveled overseas to help countries establish just laws to protect the marginalized and oppressed. Now even if you don't have many lawyers or teachers in your youth group, your students do have interests, connections, and aspirations for their own vocational pursuits. Pay attention to these. Disciple youth toward engaging with glocal issues in whatever careers they pursue, and tap their interests today as you consider how God is calling your ministry to engage locally and globally.

Pick a Place

Then choose *where* you'll most tangibly engage with this issue. While you can work for HIV/AIDS awareness and advocate for federal funding broadly, you can get to know HIV/AIDS victims in only a handful of places. The same is true for other issues we've encountered throughout the book.

You will want to choose *where* you'll most tangibly engage with this issue. One of your places has already been chosen—your own town or city. Just as there would be something wrong with seeing a mother care more deeply about other people's kids than her own, it's also wrong to see a ministry care more about poverty in Mexico while ignoring the poor in their own neighborhoods and towns. We need to view our missions and service as an extension of our local presence. If we're making little noticeable impact locally, why do we believe we can do so internationally?[5]

As you extend beyond your town's borders, don't overlook the ethnic and national connections in your own ministry. If you have exchange students from South Korea or Brazil, why not get involved in their hometowns of origin? Or if you have immigrant students, you could reach out to the communities where they came from and partner with them to respond to issues near and far.

A broadened perspective changes the way we view our own ministries, and it enhances the ways we can get involved. Keep the big picture in view and get involved with specific issues in specific places locally and globally.

Partner with the Experts

We (Dave and Terry) both have a high view of teenagers. We join with countless others who say adolescents aren't simply the church of tomorrow—they're an integral part of the church today. We've shared several examples throughout these pages regarding things we *can* do about these issues. But we shouldn't set up our students to think they alone can solve the issues of immigration, poverty, and war. While they can be part of the solution, we also need guidance from some of the organizations and experts who've devoted years of study, work, and entire careers to exploring how to best respond to the pressing issues of our world. Our service and ministry will be most fruitful when we partner with others who possess the much-needed expertise in the issues and places we tackle.

For example, imagine discovering that a significant number of your students struggle with eating disorders. It's unlikely that you'd be okay with just having a short-term mission team from overseas come in to help. You might welcome their involvement in certain ways, but if these kids were in your group, we'd hope you'd tap the best psychological and medical experts to address the issue.

The same applies to dealing with poverty, trafficking, and killer diseases. Join with organizations and experts who have invested lots of time, money, study, and experience learning how to best deal with these kinds of issues. Furthermore, nearly all of the issues we address in this book are systemic in nature. So while compassion for individuals who are diseased, trafficked, and discriminated against is appropriate, we must move beyond our acts of compassion to ask the question, "What *systemically* leads to homelessness, poverty, trafficking, etc.?" Addressing these issues at their core levels will absolutely require the skills from the kinds of organizations and experts we reference throughout these pages. They have researched and devoted their work in order to address and solve these deeper systemic issues. Young people's zeal, impressionability, and capacity for hard work and compassion combined with the help of developmental experts can bring about measureable change in our world.

Make It Mutual

Getting involved glocally inevitably includes connections that are both global and local.[6] This is one of the distinctions made between globalization and glocalization. As described in chapter 1, globalization largely benefits big corporations or other powerful bodies that develop one-way relationships to market their wares and ideas internationally. We don't have to look to MTV or Coca-Cola for examples of this. Far too many U.S. youth groups have also done this by barging into local churches overseas and taking over the ministries on their own terms. In contrast, glocalization is interested in how a local group impacts another local group, even if each is on a different side of the world.[7] This is possible because of the connections of globalization.

We sometimes need to be reminded that Westerners are not the saviors of the world. We've written our share of critiques about how that notion still permeates many missions' efforts, a situation that is improving. But there's still a tendency to make our global engagement a one-way street: *Here's what we have to offer the world.* As we note earlier, the church is growing at a rapid rate in many places around the world. Often the churches in Ecuador and Mozambique are growing faster and engaging their local communities more effectively than many churches in the U.S. and the U.K. That doesn't mean Western churches have nothing to offer; rather there are resources and needs on both sides of the relationship—it has to be mutual.

What does it look like to develop equally enriching relationships glocally—suburban churches with inner-city churches, youth groups in Atlanta with youth groups in Sao Paulo, rural youth ministries with nearby churches where seasonal farming workers attend? Let's say your group commits to a long-term relationship with a youth group in Quito. You might initially take your students to join the Quito group in building an addition to its church or sponsor a weeklong children's camp. In turn, the Quito youth group might teach your students what it means to be a Christ-follower in Quito or how to start a handcraft business to support a cause. Or, if you want to do something really different—raise the money so the Ecuadorian students can come to the U.S. to help your youth group put on a camp. Maybe together you can talk about how the way Americans eat and drink affects the Ecuadorian farmers and their families. Share what you're both learning about walking through the challenges of adolescence. Learn what it means to slow down in a more Latino style and not let the frenzy of life get the best of you. There's so much that you can learn and share together!

Over the last several years, a number of youth ministries have partnered with International Teams in Costa Rica to develop mutually beneficial partnerships. Here's what a five-year partnership has looked like for one church in Rockford, Illinois.

- Year 1: Rockford youth group travels to Costa Rica to help a local church start a youth ministry there. The Illinois students share their testimonies in Costa Rican public schools, where it's seen as a cultural exchange. As a result, several Tico (Costa Rican) students trust Christ and become the first members of a new youth group.
- Year 2: The Tico students travel to Rockford (largely funded by the Rockford group) and share their testimonies in Rockford public schools in Spanish classes where it's seen as a cultural exchange. The Tico visitors help the Rockford group reach out to new peers.
- Year 3: The Rockford group returns to Costa Rica and helps the Tico youth group set up a youth leadership team.
- Year 4: The Tico group travels to Rockford to teach some of the things they've been learning about a powerful prayer ministry.
- Year 5: Both groups travel together to Nicaragua to start the process all over again. The Tico group now lives out a five-year relationship with the Nicaraguan group that mirrors its relationship with the Illinois group.

Creative ideas are endless. Some groups have developed three-way partnerships between themselves, a youth group in Mexico, and a Latino church in their own community. These kinds of partnerships can be incredible discipleship tools for all the churches involved. Tap into the benefit of reciprocal relationships with brothers and sisters in Christ locally and globally.

Cultivate Culturally Intelligent Relationships

Youth ministry has been exemplary when it comes to realizing the importance of relationships. We know that reading books about adolescents, sequestering ourselves in the library, or stalking a few students on Facebook isn't going to cut it. Without regular life-on-life interaction with students, little impact is made. The best way to engage in students' lives is by spending time with them, seeking to understand them, and expressing the particulars of faith to them in ways that connect with their cultural understandings.

The same is true as it relates to our glocal engagement. Those of us coming from task-oriented cultures can overemphasize the "checklist": Going in and cleaning up a city park, painting a building in Mexico, and helping rebuild New Orleans. Those tasks are part of how we serve, but without relationships they're almost as bad as a youth pastor who doesn't build relationships with students. Real-life ministry happens up close.

The challenge is that many of the relationships built in glocal ministry bring us in contact with people coming from very different cultural backgrounds. Therefore some measure of cultural understanding is essential if we're going to relate to individuals in loving and respectful ways. While becoming experts on every culture we encounter is impossible, most of us can gain a measure of understanding about the dozens of different cultures we engage with each week, especially when we include not only ethnic and national cultures but also organizational and generational cultures. Your church, denomination, high school, elder board, drama club, athletic teams, and more all represent various cultures we experience in a regular week of youth ministry.

Most youth workers have a leg up on other ministry leaders when it comes to the importance of cultural understanding. It's what we do all the time. We're bridge-builders between the Bible and adolescents, parents and kids, and techie students and jocks. We try to keep current on important pop-culture trends so we can more effectively connect with our students. We need to apply this same priority and skill set to our work in various cultures that we encounter because of our glocal work. Check out some of the resources on cultural intelligence (CQ), a simple, proven way to becoming more loving, respectful, and effective as we interact with the various cultures we encounter day in, day out.[8] One of the best ways to be part of lasting change is combining cultural intelligence with the things learned from experts who have spent time studying the issue you're attempting to address.

Connect with "Big" Church

As we discern what issues to address—and where and with whom—we need to ensure we include our local church leaders as part of the process. This is especially true for local church youth ministries, but it's also true for youth workers serving with groups such as Young Life and YFC. The inevitable question becomes: *What are we supposed to do if the rest of our church is still stuck in the idea that missions is just something we support other people to do?* Start the conversation with key church leaders about their own visions for glocal mission near and far. If possible, integrate the youth ministry's efforts with the church's efforts. Everyone's work will be better for it.

If there's little vision for this among the church leadership, start small with your own group. Take one issue that impacts people both at home and in a key location overseas and begin to engage there. Or maybe you just need to start talking about the global-local connections between the ministries your youth group is already involved in. Explain to your students that missions is a whole-life endeavor, not just something they "do" when they're on a once-a-year trip to Mexico. In other words, going glocal doesn't necessarily have to involve a complete restructuring of your students' missions involvement. Start with one issue and let it grow through the relationships and responsibilities that already exist in your group.

FINAL THOUGHTS

James Macpherson, publisher of a newspaper in Pasadena, California, concluded that his U.S. staff were overpaid and under-competent. He figured he could find better, cheaper help. So he put an ad on Craigslist India seeking employees who would be based in India but report on local news in Pasadena, California. Many have pointed to Macpherson's success with this journalistic approach, but others aren't so sure. Said Joe Cutbirth, a journalism professor at Columbia University, "I don't think anyone in India could have reported on Hurricane Katrina, for example . . . You have to be on the ground. Landing in Baghdad and telling people how it is down there is reporting. Sitting at your computer in New Delhi and writing or blogging what the Defense Secretary said about it is just stenography."[9]

In the same way, we can't "outsource" our missional engagement—but neither can we do it alone. We can make a difference up close and far away. And we can partner with Christians everywhere.

The availability of global connections brings both opportunities and challenges. What a wonderful thing that so many youth groups have real-life relationships with students in other countries. But loving Mexican peers in Ensenada and ignoring or mocking Mexican classmates at home is unacceptable. The solution is to commit to a glocal response.

RESOURCES

Globalizing Theology, ed. by Craig Ott and Harold A. Netland (Baker, 2006).

Glocalization: How Followers of Jesus Engage a Flat World by Bob Roberts (Zondervan, 2007).

Discovering Missions by Charles R. Gailey and Howard Culbertson (Beacon Hill Press, 2007).

The New Global Mission by Samuel Escobar (InterVarsity, 2003).

Transformation: How Glocal Churches Transform Lives and the World by Bob Roberts, Jr. (Zondervan, 2006).

Bob Roberts/Northwood Church blog and glocal church model resources (www.glocal.net).

CHAPTER 13

15 YEAR OLDS CHANGING THE WORLD

USA Today recently ran a special section titled "Sharing in the USA."[1] The cover photo caption reads: "The new face of giving." It isn't a photo of Bill Gates, Angelina Jolie, or Oprah. It's an image of a 13-year-old kid—Josh Hofing—who took his bar mitzvah money and started a volunteer fund-raising effort that raised more than $40,000 to construct a water well in Ethiopia.

This is inspiring but not necessarily surprising to those of us who work with youth. Week in and week out we observe the burning desire of adolescents to make a difference in the world. Many times they'll be ahead of us in understanding and responding to the kinds of global issues we address in this book. (But it's nice to see a mainstream media outlet like *USA Today* acknowledge this reality!)

Most of our students might not be catalysts for raising $40,000 anytime soon, but many of them *will* jump at the chance to reach beyond borders. And when we disciple them toward caring for the world now, $40,000 might be chump change compared to the sizable impact they'll make as they pursue their adult lives and careers in the coming decades.

This final chapter begins by considering what teenagers can really do to make a difference beyond the borders of your ministry. Then we offer some guidelines for how to shape and channel their capacities for making a difference near and far.

WHAT DIFFERENCE CAN A TEENAGER MAKE?

History is filled with examples of people who did globally significant things as youth. Just look at the Scriptures. We have the familiar examples of Samuel, David, Josiah, Esther, Timothy, and many of the disciples who were making a world of difference before they reached age 20. (Or imagine what father would intentionally entrust his only child to a teenage mother? God did.)

Alexander the Great founded his first colony by the time he was 16, and Pope John XII was only 18 when his papacy began in 955. Joan of Arc accomplished all her great feats on behalf of the French before she was executed at age 20, and Mary Shelley wrote *Frankenstein* at 19.

Granted, most of us won't be dealing with students who start colonies, become Popes, or write classic novels. Many of the teenagers who fill our youth rooms each week are socially awkward, self-absorbed, and make decisions about whether or not to attend a youth event based upon who else is attending. But alongside these adolescent struggles, they have God-given longings to make things right in the world. Their invincible attitudes that can get them into trouble at weekend parties are the same ones that make them believe they can actually get rid of poverty in their lifetimes.

While most of us adults watched the impact of Hurricane Katrina with paralyzed horror, 10-year-old Talia Leman was "naïve" enough to believe she could actually do something about it. She started a fundraising campaign that led to various groups working together to raise $10 million. And Jaime Colman was a teenager when she discovered a significant need for shoes in Kenya. So she started "Walk Humbly," an effort to send 150 pairs of shoes to help the cause, and ended up with more than 4,000.[2] Many of us have heard of Zach Hunter who started "Loose Change to Loosen Chains" when he was 12, a project that harnesses our random coins just lying around to obliterate human trafficking.[3] And Jordan Foxworthy grew up a privileged kid in a show-biz family, but at age 14 she started the Bite Back Campaign to challenge her peers to give $10 to buy mosquito nets to save people from malaria. More than a half million dollars later, Jordan continues to champion her cause.

The stories continue in your youth group and ours. The role of youth in revolutions and global impact has been a recurring theme throughout history. It continues to happen today. While many of us feel overwhelmed by the issues and statistics referenced in books like this one, our youth are crazy enough to believe they can actually do something about it. Listen to their dreams, breathe life into them, and disciple them to make a world of difference.

BREATHING LIFE INTO TEENAGERS' DREAMS

Austin Gutwein is another example of a kid who dreamed about making the world a better place, and he's doing it. He used his love for basketball as a way to help AIDS orphans in Africa. A few years ago Austin decided to shoot 2,057 free throws on World AIDS Day to symbolize the number of African kids who would become AIDS orphans during Austin's school day. He asked people to sponsor him, and he raised more than $3,000. By age 14 Austin started Hoops of Hope, which to date has built two medical clinics, a lab, a school, and a water system. When you talk with Austin's parents, it's not hard to see why Hoops of Hope has become a reality. His parents are quick to defer any credit and insist they had nothing to do with it. But they also were very intentional about not squashing Austin's dream. In fact, Austin's dad is troubled by the number of parents and churches that squash kids' dreams. "Teenagers are usually told that the church is already involved in a variety of mission efforts," he said. "There has to be a way to blend the church's strategic plans with what God plants into the hearts of its youth."[4]

People assume Austin's parents did a lot of the work to get Hoops of Hope started. But his mom and dad insist it was all Austin's idea and doing. When asked about what they did to help Austin, his dad said, "We didn't say no." As Austin's parents provided guidance and assistance, they breathed life into his dream.

This is the tension: Students will be motivated to make a difference when you expose them to the needs of the world. What will you do when they approach you with those dreams?

The world of adolescents is tightly controlled and organized by adults. Fewer kids play together on their own; instead they participate in community soccer leagues run by adults. Parents hover over their teens' music lessons and homework, drive them from one practice to the next, and help them choose college courses. In the midst of this highly controlled parent-teen culture, it's easy to squash the dreams and passions of what students themselves want. And we usually do this unintentionally or unknowingly. So take special care to pay attention to their ideas and dreams. They're capable of significant work near and far. Many of them are just looking for your permission and support to be God's agents in meeting needs tugging at their hearts.

Now while these are pleasant-sounding ideals, the question is, what does it *really* look like to respond to the dreams of our youth while also realizing we can't be involved in everything? This clear tension is one that Derry Prenkert—student ministries pastor at Nappanee Missionary Church in northern Indiana—has been wrestling with over the last few years. Like most youth pastors, Derry began to think about how to get kids more engaged globally without always having to embark on short-term mission trips. He was struggling with the stewardship of spending $50,000 a year to take kids to Mexico and wondering how much impact was really being made. Furthermore, these trips involved only a small segment of the entire group of students under his care. "I wanted to see how I could get 5th and 6th graders to connect with global issues," he said, "but I also wanted to get all of the students be a part of something bigger than themselves."[5]

Derry began a three-year process to develop some long-term partnerships that could be part of the student ministry throughout the year. For example, one partnership was with a Rwandan ministry. The Rwandan group and Derry's group exchanged photos, videos, and descriptions of their lives and testimonies. Derry took time to let his students really imagine life in a place like Rwanda, and before long, they insisted on doing something more. They did some fundraisers to provide financial support, but the students wanted the rest of the congregation to be as riveted with the blessings and challenges of people living in Rwanda as they were. And that started them on a long adventure of motivating and educating the rest of the church about life for people in Rwanda and ways to live out the gospel in response to that information.

At times Derry finds himself in a quandary of remaining in sync with the church's overall vision and missional direction while also wanting to help his students dream big dreams. "I've learned not to initially say 'no' to our students' dreams," he said. "But the reality is that I can't say 'yes' every time. So I've learned to say something like, 'Show me how serious you are and write a proposal.' That begins to test the strength of their passion to pursue their dreams."

What does it look like for you to intentionally organize your ministry as a place where youth gain an imagination for making a difference in the world? In talking with people like Derry and many other youth workers, there are a few important things to remember as we breathe life into the dreams of youth:

Begin with exposure. As noted previously in these pages, you can't care about something you don't know about. This is largely why we wrote this book—to enhance your awareness of some of the emerging issues facing this and future generations. So expose your students to the needs of the world—both those in your own community and those around the world. This is one of the greatest benefits of short-term mission trips, but it doesn't happen automatically. We have to find intentional ways to expose our groups to both the blessings and challenges facing people in the places we visit. Therefore, consider teaching about these issues, using them as application points when you're studying the Scriptures together, and finding creative ways to help youth identify with the needs of their peers at home and around the globe.

Encourage first (and then listen well). As we expose our youth to the world's needs, inevitably some of them will want to do something in response. This is almost guaranteed. But often we discourage youth's enthusiastic ideas to do something because it seems unrealistic, or we just don't have the capacity to take on something else. These may be fair reservations, but at least start by encouraging your students. Commit to praying about it with them. Many times their primary reason for sharing an idea with you comes from a desperate desire to have you *simply listen*. They're often nervous and scared to talk about it out loud and curious to see if you'll respond with rolled eyes (as most adults often do when teenagers express their big dreams).

Provide direction. In time, help them channel their excitement to the hard work of actually responding. Encourage them to do some research on the issue. Make sure the cause trumps any specific ideas for how to respond. Sometimes students will get more excited about fundraising programs or events than the particular issues or actual causes. Increase their effectiveness and commitment by pointing them in the direction of where they can get more information. Breathe life into their dreams by giving them some next steps to help them continue to explore their dreams.

Let them organize it. This is crucial. Don't let adults control these ideas. Let your students do it, drive it, and lead it. Then you'll find out if it's real—and it'll be accomplished in ways that show their fingerprints of creativity. Provide direction along the way—but be sure this is their cause and event.

Create awareness through the events. Raising money isn't the primary purpose, though obviously that's a key part of responding. The larger goal is discipling others to live as God's ambassadors in the world. We can only do that by developing the global awareness and engagement of students and adults. This allows us to have an impact upon our students' responses long after they leave our youth ministries.

Beware the glamour factor. It's *en vogue* to be involved in global issues and less common to be involved at home. We've said this many times, but we want to repeat it once more: It's easy to engage with needs "over there," but what about needs closer to home? Therefore develop a glocal emphasis whenever you talk about various issues and causes.

Keep the long-term impact in view. As with anything we do in youth ministry, often we won't get to see the full scope of our impact for a long time, if ever—at least not on this side of eternity. Raising money to help with an issue today is measurable and worthy of our investment; but the impact of giving students an imagination to choose careers in light of some of our world's greatest needs—though we might not see the results as easily or quickly—has the potential to do far more good than raising $50,000.

Your response to your students' wide-eyed dreams to change the world has a huge impact on whether their dreams become a reality. When a student walks up and tells you she has a really cool way to get more clean water to people in the Congo, put down your smart phone, look her in the eye, and be fully present.

A WORD OF CAUTION

While breathing life into our students' dreams, we're wise to keep our motives in check. This is one of the issues we've often critiqued regarding some short-term mission efforts where the orientation for global service seems far too oriented around the adventure motif. Volcano hikes, island encounters, and jungle treks are all ways that some groups have attempted to recruit short-term mission teams. Most of the short-term mission projects we observe these days don't incorporate this mindset as a predominant orientation. But youth (and adults!) are still susceptible to an unhealthy motivation behind our global engagement, whether that means raising funds for HIV/AIDS orphans, organizing Bible clubs for local children, or going on short-term mission trips to Mexico.

If we aren't careful, even the best of intentions to serve globally can mix with self-serving agendas—motives that are more about making ourselves feel good than expressing Christ's love. Sometimes high school students desperately look for significance and, as a result, pour themselves into global causes to find meaning. To a certain extent that's encouraging. Taken too far, however, it can exploit people in harrowing circumstances only so we feel better about ourselves. This is the point we raised in the last chapter—ensuring that our glocal service and outreach is mutual—partnering with other Christians near and far to make a difference.

To remedy this, find ways to talk respectfully about the people and issues you're concerned about. Often the tendency is to focus so heavily on others' desperation that we end up dehumanizing them. For example, youth groups may report on short-term mission trips by talking only about their huge impacts in destitute places—the emphasis on the hopeless circumstances of the people they encountered rather than the good *and* bad that exist where they went. Youth leaders have to look for ways to intentionally highlight both sides of the story. Let love—love for God, love for the world, and love for people—drive you and your students.

Finally, despite the title of this chapter ("15 Year Olds Changing the World"), *ultimately only God changes the world.* Therefore we should respond to God's prompting and encourage our students to do the same. God's work in the world often involves the hands and feet of God's people—so surely God's world-changing happens in and through us. But there's a danger in becoming too impressed with ourselves and what we can do to eliminate poverty, racism, and other issues we've addressed in this book.

World changing is for God to do. But God invites us to join along the way to do our part.[6] Lasting change happens as people encounter Jesus up close through other individuals in real places with real issues, one day at a time.

FINAL THOUGHTS

Barbara Vogel, a fifth-grade teacher in Aurora, Colorado, believes in the power of youth to make the world a better place. She continually seeks ways to help her students understand global realities. A few years ago she read an article to her class about slavery in Sudan. The students were incited to action. They decided they wanted to buy back some of the slaves and began raising money by selling lemonade, T-shirts, and used toys. They wrote a letter to the editor of the local newspaper, and it eventually grabbed the attention of *CBS Evening News*, which in turn led to donations of $50,000. They also began an awareness campaign writing letters to national and international leaders urging them to end slavery in Sudan. "My goal is to show the power of children," Vogel said, "to show that children want to help, and to show adults what children can do."[7]

Many other kids have gotten involved in the Sudan crisis, too. Larissa started raising money to help Darfur refugees when she was 10. "You have to stand up for what is right and fight for what you believe in," she says. "No matter how young or old you are, you can make a difference if you put your heart into it."[8] For several years Larissa has used as many school assignments as possible to learn and share more about the Sudan crisis. She sold her massive Barbie collection and organized garage sales to raise additional funds. Her imagination was captured with something that matters.

History shows us that when power is threatened, students are feared most. In the midst of coups, dictators shut down universities before anything else is shut down. Just look at the revolutions that took place at the Berlin Wall, in Tiananmen Square, or during the 2009 Iranian elections to get a glimpse of the powerful way students can influence governments and media.

The topics we've covered in this book will change and grow in the coming years. They also will press upon the borders of your youth ministry. No longer can youth ministries insulate themselves from the issues of the world—they're here now. But as we learn about these realities, teach our students about them, and jointly respond, we also tap into the essence of our humanity—living as God's presence in the world.

RESOURCES

Deep Justice in a Broken World: Helping Your Kids Serve Others and Right the Wrongs Around Them by Chap Clark and Kara Powell (Zondervan/YS, 2008).

Generation Change by Zach Hunter (Zondervan/YS, 2008).

Amazing Kids! (amazing-kids.org).

RandomKid (randomkid.org).

What Kids Can Do (www.whatkidscando.org).

Bite Back (www.biteback.net).

Hoops of Hope (www.hoopsofhope.org).

EPILOGUE

We first met at a youth ministry educators' conference several years ago. There was an immediate chemistry due to our shared interests in credible research, theology, and people who work with youth. We both did doctoral dissertations on short-term missions that led us to some similar discoveries. But we each explored different emphases that mirror the areas where we continue to teach and write (Dave on cultural intelligence and global issues; Terry on ministry leadership and adolescent culture). We both serve in our local churches, have kids who are teenagers, and have the chance to write, teach, and work internationally.

But few things test a friendship like taking on a writing project together. At times I (Terry) was concerned we were being too political, and I (Dave) was concerned there wasn't enough edge. But together our greatest concern was that this book would help you and your youth respond to the global issues of our day.

What can we do? Over the next decade many of the students sitting in your youth room will be raising their own families, slogging it out in the workplace, and serving in a local church. By giving them a strong understanding of how their faith intersects with the world, you may be influencing many of the corporations, hospitals, classrooms, and governments of the future. Don't underestimate the worldwide influence your ministry can have in this way.

Which one of your students might head toward a career in business and forge a new way of partnering with workers in Mexico that isn't exploitive but brings about the hope of Jesus by way of opportunities? Who will be the filmmakers and authors who produce compelling stories that gain global audiences? What students will become the teachers who ensure the young minds in their classrooms are aware of the atrocities going on in other parts of the world rather than simply being up on the latest gossip about Hollywood? Who are the future pastors in your group who will equip their congregations to engage globally through their own families and work? And who will be the faithful factory workers who talk with love and respect to the immigrants standing beside them on the assembly lines rather than getting frustrated with their broken English?

God bless you as you reach beyond the borders of your comfort zone and prepare your students to be the presence of Christ in the world. We look forward to experiencing the worldwide implications of your faithfulness!

ENDNOTES

INTRODUCTION

1. Mike Celizic, "Miss South Carolina Teen USA Explains Herself," *Today* on MSNBC.com, August 27, 2008, http://www.msnbc.msn.com/id/20473692.
2. Rick Shenkman, *Just How Stupid Are We?: Facing the Truth about the American Voter* (New York: Basic Books, 2008), 13.

CHAPTER 1

Globalization: What in the World Matters?

1. Thomas Friedman, *The World Is Flat: A Brief History of the Twenty-First Century* (New York: Farrar, Straus & Giroux, 2005).
2. U.S. Census Bureau. World POP Clock Projection, http://www.census.gov/main/www/popclock.html (accessed February 12, 2011).
3. Donella Meadows, "Who Lives in the Global Village?" Technical Report (Hartland, Vermont: Sustainability Institute, 2005).
4. Bryant Myers, *Walking with the Poor: Principles and Practices of Transformational Development* (Maryknoll, NY: Orbis Books, 1999), 72.
5. Shawn Tully, "Teens: The Most Global Market of All." *Fortune*, May 16, 1994: 90-97.

6. Internet World Stats: Usage and Population Statistics, *Internet Usage Statistics: The Internet Big Picture*, http://www.internetworldstats.com/stats.htm.
7. Jennifer Gidley, "Global Youth Culture: A Transdisciplinary Perspective," in *Youth Futures: Comparative Research and Transformative Visions*, ed. J. Gidley and S. Inayatullah (Westport, CT: Praeger, 2002) 50-56.
8. The problems emerge after high school. When we factor in the 19-to-24-year-old age group, the risky behaviors rise significantly.
9. Center for Disease Control, 2008, *Trends in the Prevalence of Selected Risk Behaviors for All Students National YRBS: 1991-2007. http://www.cdc.gov/yrbss*
10. Stacy Teciher Khadaroo, "U.S. High School Graduation Rate Climbs to 69.2 Percent," The Christian Science Monitor (June 9, 2009), http://www.csmonitor.com/USA/2009/0609/p02s13-usgn.html (accessed February 9, 2011).
11. J.J. Arnett, *Adolescence and Emerging Adulthood: A Cultural Approach*. (Upper Saddle River, NJ: Prentice Hall, Inc., 2001).
12. See Chap Clark's *Hurt: Inside the World of Teenagers* (Grand Rapids: Baker Books, 2004) for research on some of the challenges of extended adolescence in the U.S.
13. T. Linhart and D. Livermore, *Global Youth Ministry* (Grand Rapids, MI: Zondervan/Youth Specialties Academic, 2011).
14. David Barrett and Todd Johnson, eds., *World Christian Trends: AD 30-AD 2200* (Pasadena, CA: William Carey Library, 2001).
15. Philip Jenkins, *The Next Christendom: The Coming of Global Christianity* (New York: Oxford University Press, 2002), 37.
16. Dave discussed this phenomenon in greater detail in "One Church: The Changing Face of Christianity" in David Livermore, *Serving with Eyes Wide Open* (Grand Rapids: Baker Books, 2006), 31-42.
17. Adapted from Peter Unger, *Living High and Letting Die: Our Illusion of Innocence* (New York: Oxford University Press, 1996) 136-139.

CHAPTER 2

The View Across the Aisle: Understanding Our Reactions

1. David Livermore, *Cultural Intelligence: Improving Your CQ to Engage Our Multicultural World* (Grand Rapids: Baker Books, 2009), 232.
2. Richard Rohr, *Everything Belongs: The Gift of Contemplative Prayer* (New York: Crossroad Publishing, 2003), 31.
3. This is opposite of how many would believe it should be, yet global travel (including short-term mission trips) have been shown to sometimes produce

greater ethnocentricity and *greater* materialistic habits. It's not automatic that if you travel the world, you'll become more globally sensitive or missions-minded.

4. David Livermore, *Cultural Intelligence*, 182-86.
5. Richard Cunningham, "Theologizing in a Global Context: Changing Contours," *Review and Expositor* 94 (1997), 359.
6. John Franke, "Still the Way, Truth, and the Life," *Christianity Today* (December 2009), 31.
7. For material on developing a deeper, theological response, see Chap Clark and Kara Powell's *Deep Justice in a Broken World: Helping Your Kids Serve Others and Right the Wrongs around Them* (Grand Rapids: Zondervan/YS, 2007) and David Livermore, *What Can I Do?: Making a Global Difference Right Where You Are* (Grand Rapids: Zondervan, 2010).

CHAPTER 3

"Me? Rich? Yeah, Right!": Poverty and Hunger

1. United Nations Development Program, Human Development Report, 2007/2008 Highlights.
2. T. Linhart, "Do Short-Term Mission Trips Make a Long-Term Impact?" *Group*, 93-97 (2005); T. Linhart, "Planting Seeds: The Curricular Hope for Short-Term Mission Experience in Youth Ministry," *Christian Education Journal*, Series 3, 2(2), 256-272 (2005); T. Linhart, "They Were So Alive!: The Spectacle Self and Youth Group Short-Term Mission Trips," *Missiology*, 4, 451-462 (2006); D. Livermore, *Serving with Eyes Wide Open: Doing Short-Term Missions with Cultural Intelligence* (Grand Rapids, MI: Baker Publishing, 2006).
3. Uri Berliner, "Haves and Have-Nots: Income Inequality in America," NPR.org (February 5, 2007), http://www.npr.org/templates/story/story.php?storyId=7180618.
4. Tami Luhby, "As Income Gap Widens, Recession Fears Grow," CNNMoney.com (April 9, 2008), http://money.cnn.com/2008/04/09/news/economy/incomegap/index.htm.
5. Jodie T. Allen. "A Nation of 'Haves' and 'Have-Nots'?" Pew Research Center for the People and the Press (September 13, 2007), http://pewresearch.org/pubs/593/haves-have-nots.
6. Noelle Knox, "Wealth Gap Swallows Up American Dream," *USA Today* (November 24, 2006), http://www.usatoday.com/money/perfi/housing/2006-11-24-luxury-homes-usat_x.htm.
7. "Understanding Poverty," www.web.worldbank.org.

8. Gregg Easterbrook, *The Progress Paradox: How Life Gets Better While People Feel Worse* (New York: Random House, 2004).
9. Paul Collier, *The Bottom Billion: Why the Poorest Countries Are Failing and What Can Be Done About It* (New York: Oxford University Press) 2007, 6.
10. See *www.lifestraw.com*
11. William Easterly, *The White Man's Burden* (New York: Penguin Books, 2006), 369.
12. Don Cheadle and John Prendergast, *Not on Our Watch: The Mission to End Genocide in Darfur and Beyond* (New York: Hyperion, 2007), 101.

CHAPTER 4

Silent Killers: HIV/AIDS, Malaria, TB

1. Johann Le Roux and Cheryl Sylvia Smith, "Causes and Characteristics of the Street Child Phenomenon: A Global Perspective," *Adolescence* 33, no. 131 (Fall 1998) pp. 683-688.
2. Joint United Nations Programme on HIV/AIDS (UNAIDS) and World Health Organization (WHO), AIDS Epidemic Update, December 2007, Switzerland, 2007, http://data.unaids.org/pub/EPISlides/2007/2007_epiupdate_en.pdf.
3. Abana Jean-Paul, "Rwandese Children with HIV/AIDS Share Their Stories," MSF.org.
4. M. Glynn, et al. "Estimated HIV prevalence in the United States at the End of 2003." National HIV Prevention Conference; June 12-15, 2005; Atlanta. Abstract T1-B1101.
5. Jehangir S. Pocha, "Letter from China: Where Heroin Glows, an AIDS Explosion," *The Boston Globe*, June 8, 2006.
6. William Easterly, *The White Man's Burden: Why the West's Efforts to Aid the Rest Have Done So Much Ill and So Little Good* (New York: Penguin Books, 2006), 252.
7. Ibid., 249.
8. Ibid., 255.
9. By including "C" we are *not* advocating unfaithfulness or promiscuous life-styles; we're just reporting what the ABC program reported.
10. Rob Cheeley, HIV-AIDS Report: 15 Years in Uganda, Kunming, China: Bless China, April 2008.
11. Epidemiological Country Profile on HIV and AIDS: China, World Health Organization, China, http://www.who.int/countries/chn/en (accessed February 12, 2011).

CHAPTER 5

Sex and Soldiers for Sale: Human Trafficking

1. Kevin Bales, *Disposable People: New Slavery in the Global Economy* (Los Angeles, CA: University of California Press, 1999), 9.
2. U.S. Department of State Office to Monitor and Combat Trafficking in Persons, "U.S. Department of State: Trafficking in Persons Report" (June 4, 2008), http://www.state.gov/g/tip/rls/tiprpt/2008/105376.htm.
3. Coalition to Stop the Use of Child Soldiers, http://www.child-soldiers.org/childsoldiers/child-soldiers.
4. Polaris Project: For a World without Slavery, http://www.polarisproject.org.
5. Caitlin O'Neil, "Sex Trafficking Hits Close to Home," http://www.thelantern.com/campus/sex-trafficking-hits-close-to-home-60-90-women-affected-in-franklin-county-1.890395 (accessed February 9, 2011).
6. Nea Zoi, Association for the Support and Restoration of Individuals in Prostitution, http://neazoi.org.
7. U.S. Department of State, Office to Monitor and Combat Trafficking in Persons, http://www.state.gov/g/tip.
8. "Campaign Against Child Trafficking in the Chocolate Industry," Stop the Traffik, http://www.stopthetraffik.org/ourwork/chocolate.

CHAPTER 6

Techno-Craziness: Technology and Media

1. Kurt Bensmiller, *Truly, Madly, Deeply Engaged: Global Youth, Media and Technology* (2006). Available online at http://us.yimg.com/i/adv/tmde_05/truly_madly_final_booklet.pdf.
2. The Nielsen Company, *How Teens Use Media: A Nielsen Report on the Myths and Realities of Teen Media Trends* (June 2009). Available online at http://blog.nielsen.com/nielsenwire/reports/nielsen_howteensusemedia_june09.pdf.
3. Ruth Mortimer, "Global Youth and Technology Trends from MTV, Nickelodeon, and Microsoft," Brand & Business Blog (July 25, 2007), http://brandstrategy.wordpress.com/2007/07/25/global-youth-and-technology-trends-from-mtv-nickelodeon-and-microsoft (accessed February 11, 2011).
4. Mizuko Ito, et al., *Living and Learning with New Media: Summary of Findings from the Digital Youth Project*, MacArthur Foundation (November 2008).

Retrieved from www.macfound.org/atf/cf/.../DML_ETHNOG_WHITE PAPER.PDF.

5. Amanda Lenhart, "More and More Teens on Cell Phones." Pew Research Center Publications (August 2009) http://pewresearch.org/pubs/1315/teens-use-of-cell-phones.
6. David Rock, *Your Brain at Work* (New York: Harper Collins, 2009), 36.
7. Jennifer Gidley, "Global Youth Culture: A Transdisciplinary Perspective," in *Youth Futures: Comparative Research and Transformative Visions*, ed. J. Gidley and S. Inayatullah (Westport, CT: Praeger, 2002), 9.
8. The National Campaign to Prevent Teen and Unplanned Pregnancy, "Teens, Sex and Technology, What's Really Going On" (February 10, 2009), http://www.opposingviews.com/i/teens-sex-and-technology-what-s-really-going-on.
9. Alexandria Rankin Macgill, *Parents, Teens and Technology*, PewResearchCenter Publications (October 2007), http://pewresearch.org/pubs/621/parents-teens-and-technology.
10. "Calling Freedom: How Mobile Phones May Help to Deter Kidnaps," *The Economist* (December 19, 2009), 60.

CHAPTER 7

"Hug a Tree?!": Caring for the Environment

1. Thomas Kostigen, *You Are Here: Exposing the Vital Link Between What We Do and What That Does to Our Planet* (New York: Harper Collins, 2008), 143-44.
2. Tim Sanders, *Saving the World at Work: What Companies and Individuals Can Do to Go Beyond Making a Profit to Making a Difference* (New York: Doubleday, 2008), 33.
3. Amitav Ghosh, *The Hungry Tide* (Boston: Houghton Mifflin, 2005), 249.
4. Seeing Green, *The World in 2008* (London: Economist Intelligence Unit, 2008), 52.
5. Anthony Hoekema, *Created in God's Image* (Grand Rapids: Eerdmans, 1986), 80.
6. NICEF, "Progress for Children: A World Fit for Children," *Statistical Review* 6 (December 2007), 40.
7. Peter Singer, One World (New Haven, CT: Yale University Press, 2002), 31 and Keep America Beautiful, "Waste Reduction and Recycling," http://www.kab.org/site/PageServer?pagename=Focus_Waste_reduction (accessed February 10, 2011).
8. Some of these ideas were adapted from http://www.princeton.edu/~greening (accessed February 10, 2011).

9. www.energystar.gov.
10. N.T. Wright, *What Saint Paul Really Said: Was Paul of Tarsus the Real Founder of Christianity?* (Grand Rapids: Eerdmans, 1997), 154.

CHAPTER 8

Invaded by Aliens: Immigration

1. The Karen are a people group in southeast Asia, particularly in Myanmar/Burma, Thailand, and Laos.
2. Churches' Commission for Migrants in Europe, http://www.ccme.be.
3. BBC News, "Global Migrants Reach 191 Million" (June 7, 2006), http://news.bbc.co.uk/2/hi/americas/5054214.stm.
4. Taken from "A Quick Look at U.S. Immigrants: Demographics, Workforce, and Asset-Building," by The Immigrant Policy Project of the National Conference of State Legislatures (June 17, 2004). Accessed February 12, 2011 from: http://www.ncsl.org/Default.aspx?TabId=13146.
5. Tony Carnes, "The Peoples Are Here: Record Immigration Pushes Christians Out of Their Comfort Zone," *Christianity Today*, posted February 1, 2003, http://www.christianitytoday.com/ct/2003/february/10.76.html (accessed February 11, 2011).
6. Ibid.
7. Taken from "A Quick Look at U.S. Immigrants."
8. Steven A. Camarota, "Immigrants in the United States—2002: A Snapshot of America's Foreign-Born Population," *Backgrounder*, a publication of the Center for Immigration Studies (November 2002), 20. http://ww.cis.org/articles/2002/back1302.html.
9. Jack Gladstone, "The New Population Bomb," *Foreign Affairs 89*, 1 (January/February 2010), 42-43.
10. World Relief has posted some denominations' stances on its Web site (http://worldrelief.org/Page.aspx?pid=1524).
11. Daniel B. Wood, "Churches Resist Tougher Immigration Laws," *Christian Science Monitor* (March 14, 2006) http://www.csmonitor.com/2006/0314/p01s01-ussc.html.
12. See Amie Steffen, "Faith Leaders Unite to Support Immigration Reform,"http://wcfcourier.com/news/local/article_dc42519b-994f-53dc-ab77-4bee13735906.html, WFCCourier.com.
13. See Orlon Love, "Two Years After Agriprocessors Raid, Postville is Flush with New Optimism" at http://thegazette.com/2010/05/12/two-years-after-agriprocessors-raid-postville-is-flush-with-new-optimism, TheGazette.com.
14. See Stephanie Condon, "Religious Leaders Mobilize Against Arizona

Immigration Law," http://www.cbsnews.com/8301-503544_162-20003812-503544.html, CBSNews.com.

15. See Dan Gilgoff, "New Force for Broad Immigration Reform: Conservative Evangelicals," http://articles.cnn.com/2010-05-10/politics/immigration.evangelicals_1_immigration-reform-latino-evangelicals-illegal-immigrants?_s=PM:POLITICS, CNN.com.
16. For example, see Richard Munoz, "Faithful Companions," *Christian Reflection: A Series in Faith and Ethics* (Center for Christian Ethics at Baylor University, 2008), 35-43. http://www.baylor.edu/christianethics/index.php?id=56774.
17. United States Conference of Catholic Bishops, Justice for Immigrants, "Countering the Myths," http://www.justiceforimmigrants.org/myths.shtml.
18. Gerald B. Kieschnick and Matthew Harrison, Joint Statement Regarding Immigration Concerns, Lutheran Church-Missouri Synod, 2006. http://www.lcms.org.
19. Matthew Soerens and Jenny Hwang, *Welcoming the Stranger: Justice, Compassion* and *Truth in the Immigration Debate* (Downers Grove, IL: IVP Press, 2009). Her quote is found at http://www.brownpride.us/forum/churches-share-nations-concern-needed-immigration-reform-t32625.html.

CHAPTER 9

Pride and Prejudice: Social Class

1. See John Blake, "Why Many Americans Prefer their Sundays Segregated," CNN.com (August 4, 2008), http://www.cnn.com/2008/LIVING/wayoflife/08/04/segregated.sundays/index.html. Also read: Curtiss Paul DeYoung, Michael O. Emerson, George Yancey, and Karen Chai Kim, *United by Faith: The Multiracial Congregation as an Answer to the Problem of Race* (New York: Oxford University Press, 2004) and Michael O. Emerson and Christian Smith, *Divided by Faith: Evangelical Religion and the Problem of Race in America* (New York: Oxford University Press, 2001).
2. bell hooks, *Where We Stand: Class Matters* (New York: Routledge, 2000).
3. Reinhard Bendix, *Max Weber: An Intellectual Portrait* (Berkeley, CA: University of California Press, 1978).
4. You can learn more at the Ohio state Web site (https://webapp1.ode.state.oh.us/cncs/view.asp?id=262779578278521386 and http://ilrc.ode.state.oh.us/Districts).
5. "55 Percent of College Students Graduate" (June 3, 2009), http://www.upi.com/Top_News/2009/06/03/55-percent-of-college-students-graduate/UPI-15671244064567.

6. Guy Debord (1995; 1998) in *The Society of the Spectacle* theorizes that the essence of modern society is the spectacle—"a social relationship between people that is mediated by images" (1995, 12) and consists of both the experiences and material structure of a society which "proclaims the predominance of appearances and asserts that all human life, which is to say all social life, is mere appearance" (14).
7. University of Illinois at Chicago, *Youth and Religion Project.* http://www.uic.edu/depts/soci/yrp/comp/pages/prode.html.

CHAPTER 10

Satan's Schemes: Ethnic Division (with Eric Iverson)

1. Joseph Daniels, "The Psychopathology of Racism," *Christianity Today* (January 15, 1971) 7-8, in *Divided by Faith* by Emerson and Smith.
2. Adapted from David Livermore, *Cultural Intelligence: Improving Your CQ to Engage Our Multicultural World* (Grand Rapids: Baker Books, 2009), 95.
3. U.S. Census Bureau, http://quickfacts.census.gov/qfd/meta/long_68184.htm.
4. U.S. Census Bureau, http://factfinder.census.gov/home/en/epss/glossary_r.html#race.
5. Thomas Jefferson, *Notes on the State of Virginia* (New York: Penguin Classics, 1998) 150-151.
6. Andrew Jackson's Fifth Annual Message, Inferior Race, December 3, 1833. http://www.synaptic.bc.ca/ejournal/JacksonFifthAnnualMessage.htm (accessed March 20, 2011).
7. *Divided by Faith*, 69.
8. Ibid., 69-70.
9. Ibid., 70.
10. Ibid., 170.
11. Adapted from David Livermore, *Cultural Intelligence*, 96-97.

CHAPTER 11

Hollywood Versus Jihad: Clash of Civilizations

1. Adapted from "Portrait of a Suicide Bomber," *The Week* (December 24, 2001), 14. (Published by Malayala Manorama Group, Kochi, Kerala, India).

2. John Piper and Justin Taylor, eds. *The Supremacy of Christ in a Postmodern World* (Wheaton, IL: Good New Publishers, 2007) 26.
3. Benjamin Barber, *Jihad vs. McWorld: How Globalism and Tribalism Are Reshaping the World* (New York: Ballantine Books, 1996) 9.
4. Sam George, "TerrorCulture: Worth Living for or Worth Dying For," in *One World or Many: The Impact of Globalisation on Mission*, ed. Richard Tiplady, 55-70 (Pasadena, CA: William Carey Publishers, 2003) 57.
5. Ibid., 58.
6. Ibid., 59.
7. Ibid., 56.
8. To begin, start with Lesslie Newbigin, *The Gospel in a Pluralist Society* (Grand Rapids, MI: Eerdmans, 1989).
9. Eboo Patel, "A Common Word vs. a Clash of Civilizations," *The Review of Faith and International Affairs*, 6, no. 4 (2008): 53.

CHAPTER 12

"Glocal Service": Making a Difference Near and Far

1. Barry Wellman and Keith Hampton, "Living Networked On and Offline," *Contemporary Sociology* 28, 6 (November 1999): 648-54.
2. Mortimer Arias, "Global and Local: A Critical View of Mission Models," *Global Good News*, Howard A. Snyder, ed. (Nashville: Abingdon, 2001), 64.
3. Charles E. Van Engen, "The Glocal Church: Locality and Catholicity in a Globalizing World," in *Globalizing Theology*, Craig Ott and Harold A. Netland, eds. (Grand Rapids, MI: Baker, 2006), 161.
4. Bob Roberts, interview with Mark Galli, "Glocal Church Ministry," *Christianity Today* (July 2007), 42-46.
5. James F. Engel and William A. Dyrness, *Changing the Mind of Missions: Where Have We Gone Wrong*? (Downers Grove: InterVarsity Press, 2000) 130.
6. John Nuessle, "The Global and the Local in Christian Mission" Mission Papers 2008 (New York: General Board of Global Ministries of the United Methodist Church, 2008) 3, http://new.gbgm-umc.org/news/themes/gc/resources/?search=global percent20local&C=5305&I=17595.
7. Ibid.
8. See Dave's books on cultural intelligence at http://davidlivermore.com/books.
9. Ravi Somaiya, "Outsourcing News: 'Glocal' Takes Off," The Guardian (London), December 8, 2008. You can see their work at www.pasadenanow.com.

CHAPTER 13

15 Year Olds Changing the World

1. Andrea Stone, "The New Face of Giving," Sharing in the USA, special section of *USA Today* (October 7, 2008).
2. http://www.therebelution.com/blog/2009/02/jaime-colman-shoes-for-karogoto.
3. http://www.freetheslaves.net/Page.aspx?pid=183.
4. Dan Gutwein, personal conversation with Terry Linhart, December 2009.
5. Derry Prenkert, personal conversation with Terry Linhart, December 2009.
6. Andy Crouch, *Culture Making: Recovering Our Creative Calling* (Downers Grove, IL: InterVarsity Press, 2008), 189.
7. Don Cheadle and John Prendergast, *Not on Our Watch: The Mission to End Genocide in Darfur and Beyond* (New York: Hyperion, 2007), 119.
8. Ibid., 162.

Share Your Thoughts

With the Author: Your comments will be forwarded to the author when you send them to *zauthor@zondervan.com.*

With Zondervan: Submit your review of this book by writing to *zreview@zondervan.com.*

Free Online Resources at

www.zondervan.com

Zondervan AuthorTracker: Be notified whenever your favorite authors publish new books, go on tour, or post an update about what's happening in their lives at www.zondervan.com/authortracker.

Daily Bible Verses and Devotions: Enrich your life with daily Bible verses or devotions that help you start every morning focused on God. Visit www.zondervan.com/newsletters.

Free Email Publications: Sign up for newsletters on Christian living, academic resources, church ministry, fiction, children's resources, and more. Visit www.zondervan.com/newsletters.

Zondervan Bible Search: Find and compare Bible passages in a variety of translations at www.zondervanbiblesearch.com.

Other Benefits: Register yourself to receive online benefits like coupons and special offers, or to participate in research.